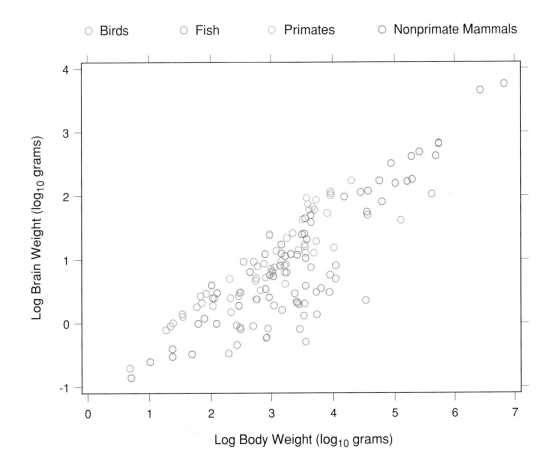

Figure I. COLOR ENCODING A CATEGORICAL VARIABLE. Color is a powerful tool that can genuinely enhance the visual decoding of information on data displays. Color can also be used to no purpose. We need to be hard-boiled in evaluating the efficacy of a visualization tool. It is easy to be dazzled by a display of data rendered in a rainbow of colors; our tendency is to be misled into thinking we are absorbing relevant information when we see a lot. But the success of a visualization tool should be based solely on the amount we learn about the phenomenon under study. There are two uses of color that genuinely transmit information from display to viewer. One is the rendering of different categories of graphical elements in different colors to provide efficient visual assembly of the categories, that is, to allow us to see each category of elements as a whole, mentally filtering out the other categories. In this figure, four different categories of plotting symbols are color encoded, and we can easily assemble the symbols of each category. The second use of color is illustrated by the display on the next page.

To my parents

Acknowledgements

To John Tukey, for ingenious inventions and applications of graphical data analysis.

To many colleagues at Bell Labs, for creating an optimal environment to study graphical data analysis.

To Marylyn McGill, for relentlessly pursuing perfection in experimenting with graphical displays.

To Bob McGill, for our experiments in graphical perception and our many experiments with graphical inventions.

To Nick Fisher, for effective communication of graphical principles based on scientific enquiry.

To Sue Pope and Tina Sharp, for the considerable word processing skills that were needed to produce the text.

To Lisa Cleveland, for days of proofreading in Summit and Abcoude.

To Estelle McKittrick, for help in many forms.

To Gerard Gorman, for the image processing that was needed to produce many of the displays.

To Alan Cossa, for a high level of quality control in producing camera-ready output.

To many who commented on the manuscript — Paul Anderson, Jon Bentley, John Chambers, Nick Cox, Lisa Cleveland, Arnold Court, Mary Donnelly, Nick Fisher, Bob Futrelle, Colin Mallows, Bob McGill, Marylyn McGill, Brad Murphy, Richard Nuccitelli, James Palmer, Arno Penzias, and John Tukey.

Published by Hobart Press, Summit, New Jersey

Copyright ©1994 AT&T. All rights reserved.

Printed in the United States of America

ISBN 0-9634884-1-4   CLOTH

LIBRARY OF CONGRESS CATALOG CARD NUMBER: 94-075052

PUBLISHER'S CATALOGING IN PUBLICATION

Cleveland, William S., 1943–
    The elements of graphing data / by William S. Cleveland.
    Revised edition.
    p. cm.
    Includes bibliographical references and index.

    1. Graphic methods.   2. Mathematical statistics–Graphic
    methods.   I. Title.

QA90.C54 1994   511′.5

Contents

Preface

This book is about visualizing data in science and technology. It contains graphical methods and principles that are powerful tools for showing the structure of data. The material is relevant for data *analysis*, when the analyst wants to study data, and for data *communication*, when the analyst wants to communicate data to others.

When a graph is made, quantitative and categorical information is encoded by a display method. Then the information is visually decoded. This visual perception is a vital link. No matter how clever the choice of the information, and no matter how technologically impressive the encoding, a visualization fails if the decoding fails. Some display methods lead to efficient, accurate decoding, and others lead to inefficient, inaccurate decoding. It is only through scientific study of visual perception that informed judgments can be made about display methods. The display methods of *Elements* rest on a foundation of scientific enquiry.

Except for one small section, there is nothing in this book about computer graphics. The basic ideas, the methods, and the principles of the book transcend the computing environment used to implement them. While graphics technology is moving along at a rapid pace, the human visual system has remained the same.

The prerequisites for understanding the book are minimal. A few topics require a knowledge of the elementary concepts of probability and statistical science, but these topics can be skipped without affecting comprehension of the remainder of the book.

The book *Visualizing Data* is a companion volume [26]. It focuses on graphical methods, the topic of Chapter 3 of this book; it presents far more methods than covered here and is more advanced, requiring a greater knowledge of statistics. But *Visualizing Data* does not delve into graphical perception, and takes *Elements* as a starting point.

Elements was meant to be read from the beginning and to be enjoyed. However, it is possible to read here and there. Winding its way through the book is a summary of the material: the figures and their legends. Reading this summary can help readers direct themselves to specific items.

The graphs in this book are communicating information about fascinating subjects, and I have not hesitated to describe the subjects in some detail when needed. In many cases some knowledge of the subject is required to understand the purpose of a graphical analysis or why a graph is not doing what was intended or what a new graphical method can show us about data. I hope the reader will share with me the excitement of experiencing the increased insight that graphical data display brings us about these subjects.

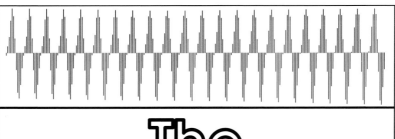

The Elements of Graphing Data

William S. Cleveland

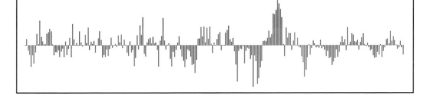

4

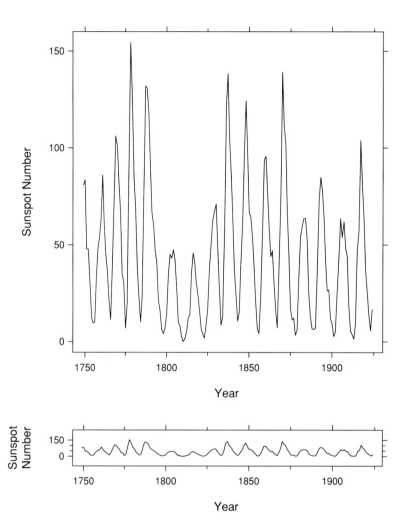

Year

Year

1.1 GRAPHICAL METHODS AND PRINCIPLES. The visualization of data requires
basic principles and methods. Both panels of this graph show the yearly sunspot
numbers from 1749 to 1924. A display method, banking to 45°, has been used to
choose the shape, or aspect ratio, of the bottom panel. The method allows us to perceive
an important property of the sunspots that is not revealed in the top panel — the
sunspots rise more rapidly than they fall.

1 Introduction

Data display is critical to data analysis. Graphs allow us to explore data to see overall patterns and to see detailed behavior; no other approach can compete in revealing the structure of data so thoroughly. Graphs allow us to view complex mathematical models fitted to data, and they allow us to assess the validity of such models.

But realizing the potential of data visualization requires methods and basic principles. Figure 1.1 illustrates this. The top panel graphs the yearly sunspot numbers from 1749 to 1924. The dominant frequency component of variation in the data is the cycles with periods of about 11 years. The existence of the cycles is clearly revealed, but an important property of them is not. And this property is critical to understanding the variation in the cycles, which in turn is critical to developing theories of solar physics that explain the origin of the sunspots. The problem is the shape, or aspect ratio, of the graph, a square. The data are graphed again in the bottom panel; a method called *banking to 45°*, which will be introduced in Chapter 2, is used to determine the aspect ratio, and the result is a narrow rectangle. Now the graph reveals the important property. The cycles typically rise more rapidly than they fall; this behavior is most pronounced for the cycles with high peaks, is less pronounced for those with medium peaks, and disappears for those cycles with the very lowest peaks.

This book is about methods and basic principles that help the data analyst to realize the potential of visualization. The next three chapters of the book divide the material into principles of graph construction, graphical methods, and graphical perception. In this chapter, Section 1.1 (pp. 6–9) demonstrates the power of visualization, Section 1.2 (pp. 9–15), demonstrates how easy it is for the graphing of data go wrong, and Section 1.3 (pp. 16–21) briefly describes the content of the next three chapters.

1.1   The Power of Graphical Data Display

Figure 1.2 illustrates the power of visualization to reveal complex patterns in data. The top left panel is a graph of monthly average atmospheric carbon dioxide concentrations measured at the Mauna Loa Observatory in Hawaii [9,71]. These data woke up the world. Charles Keeling pioneered their collection and fostered them amidst the adversity of nature at the top of a volcano and the controversy of man closer to sea level. The controversy raged first in science and then later in politics [108]. Earlier data had hinted that atmospheric CO_2 was rising due to man-made emissions, but Keeling's data proved the case, signaling the danger of global climate change.

The remaining panels of Figure 1.2 show a numerical decomposition of the data into four frequency components of variation whose sum is equal to the CO_2 concentrations. The decomposition was carried out by a statistical procedure, STL [21]. On the five vertical scales of the figure, the number of units per cm varies. The heights of the bars on the right sides of the panels provide a visualization of the relative scaling; the heights represent equal changes in parts per million on the five vertical scales.

The component graphed in the upper right panel is a trend component that describes the persistent long-term increase in the level of the concentrations. This rise, if continued unabated, will eventually cause atmospheric temperatures to rise, the polar ice caps to melt, the coastal areas of the continents to flood, and the climates of different regions of the earth to change radically [57,80,108]. And the graph shows that the rate of increase of CO_2 is itself increasing through time.

The component graphed in the third panel from the bottom is a seasonal component: a yearly cycle in the concentrations due to the waxing and waning of foliage in the Northern Hemisphere. When foliage grows in the spring, plant tissue absorbs CO_2 from the atmosphere, depositing some of the carbon in the soil, and atmospheric concentrations decline. When the foliage decreases at the end of the summer, CO_2 returns to the atmosphere, and the atmospheric concentrations increase. The graph shows that the amplitudes of these seasonal oscillations have increased slightly through time.

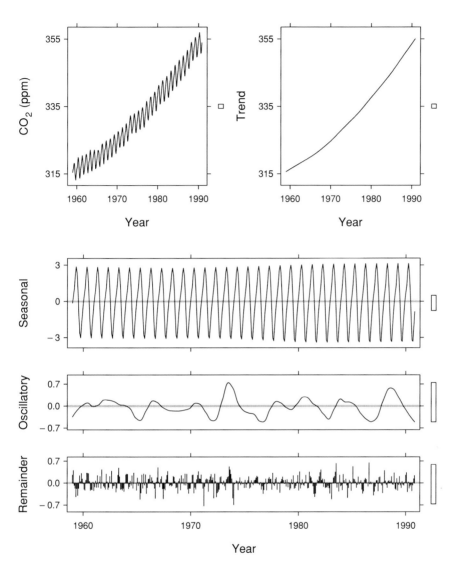

1.2 THE POWER OF GRAPHICAL DATA DISPLAY. Visualization provides insight that cannot be appreciated by any other approach to learning from data. On this graph, the top left panel displays monthly average CO_2 concentrations from Mauna Loa, Hawaii. The remaining panels show frequency components of variation in the data. The heights of the five bars on the right sides of the panels portray the same changes in ppm on the five vertical scales.

An oscillatory component, graphed in the second panel from the bottom, is made up mostly of variation with periods in a band centered near three years. This variation is associated with changes in the Southern Oscillation index, a measure of the difference in atmospheric pressure between Easter Island in the South Pacific and Darwin, Australia. Changes in the index are also associated with changes in climate. For example, when the index drops sharply, the trade winds are reduced and the temperature of the equatorial Pacific increases. This warming, which has important consequences for South America, often occurs around Christmas time and is called El Niño — the child [73].

The component shown in the bottom panel has no apparent, strong, time pattern and behaves, for the most part, like random noise.

Figure 1.2 conveys a large amount of information about the CO_2 concentrations. We have been able to summarize overall behavior and to see detailed information. As the eminent statistician W. Edwards Deming would have put it [45], "the graph retains the information in the data."

Many techniques of data analysis have data reduction as their first step. For example, classical statistical procedures, widely used in science and technology, fall in this category. The first step is to take all of the data and reduce them to a few statistics such as means, standard deviations, correlation coefficients, variance components, and t-tests. Then, inferences are based on this very limited collection of values. Using only numerical reduction methods in data analyses is far too limiting. We cannot expect a small number of numerical values to consistently convey the wealth of information that exists in data. Numerical reduction methods do not retain the information in the data.

Contained within the data of any investigation is information that can yield conclusions to questions not even originally asked. That is, there can be surprises in the data. The progress of science depends heavily on formulating hypotheses and probing them by data collection. Darwin, in a letter to Henry Fawcett in 1861, writes [54]: "How odd it is that anyone should not see that all observation must be for or against some view if it is to be of any service." But analyses of data should not narrowly focus on just those hypotheses that led to collection. This inhibits finding surprises in the data. To regularly miss surprises by failing to probe thoroughly with visualization tools is terribly inefficient because the cost of intensive data analysis is typically very small compared with the cost of data collection.

A graph of CO_2 concentrations similar to that of Figure 1.2 produced a surprise discovery. For a long time it was thought that the amplitude of the seasonal component was stable and not changing through time, but eventually three groups — one at CSIRO in Australia [102], a second at Scripps Institution of Oceanography in the United States [3], and a third at AT&T Bell Laboratories in the United States [30] — independently discovered the small, but persistent change in the Mauna Loa seasonal cycles. For the Bell Labs group, the discovery was serendipitous. The goal of the analysis had been to study the relationship between CO_2 and the Southern Oscillation index. The first step in the analysis was to decompose the CO_2 concentrations as in Figure 1.2 to get the oscillatory component so it could be correlated with the index. Fortunately, the group graphed all of the components, and the graph showed clearly the persistent change in the amplitude of the seasonal component. This surprise was so exciting that the group switched its mission to the seasonal behavior of CO_2 and abandoned the original mission. No one yet has a good understanding of what is causing the change. It might be a harbinger of changes in the earth's climate or it might be simply part of the natural variation in CO_2.

1.2   The Challenge of Graphical Data Display

Visualization is surprisingly difficult. Even the most simple matters can easily go wrong. This will be illustrated by three examples where seemingly straightforward graphical tasks ran into trouble.

Aerosol Concentrations

Figure 1.3 is a graphical method called a *q-q plot* which will be
discussed in detail in Chapter 3; the figure shows the graph as it
originally appeared in a *Science* report [31]. As with almost all of the
reproduced graphs in this book, the size of the graph is the same as that
of the source. The display compares Sunday and workday
concentrations of aerosols, or particles in the air. First, the graph has a
construction error: the 0.0 label on the horizontal scale should be 0.6.
Unfortunately, the error makes it appear that the left corner is the origin;
many readers probably wondered why the line $y = x$, which is drawn
on the graph, does not go through the origin. A second problem is that
the scales on the graph are poorly chosen; comparison of the Sunday
and workday values would have been enhanced by making the
horizontal and vertical scales the same. Scale issues such as these are
discussed in Chapter 2. Finally, the display of the data misses an
opportunity to see the behavior of the data more thoroughly. On this
single panel it is not easy to compare the vertical distances of the points
from the line $y = x$; the solution is a graphical method called the *Tukey
mean-difference plot*, which will be introduced in Chapter 3.

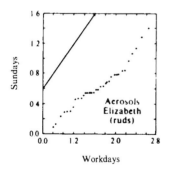

1.3 THE CHALLENGE OF GRAPHICAL DATA DISPLAY. This
graph compares Sunday and workday concentrations of aerosols.
The line shown is $y = x$. The graph has problems. There is a
construction error: the 0.0 label on the horizontal scale is wrong
and should be 0.6. The horizontal and vertical scales should be
the same but are not. Furthermore, it is hard to judge the
deviations of the points from the line $y = x$.

O-Ring Data

On January 27, 1986, the day before the last flight of the space shuttle
Challenger, a group of engineers met to study an alarm that had been
raised. The forecast of temperature at launch time the following day was
$31°$. There was a suggestion that the low temperature might affect the
performance of the O-rings that sealed the joints of the rocket motors.

To assess the issue, the engineers studied a graph of the data shown in Figure 1.4. Each data point was from a shuttle flight in which the O-rings had experienced thermal distress. The horizontal scale is O-ring temperature, and the vertical scale is the number of O-rings experiencing distress. The graph revealed no effect of temperature on the number of stress problems, and Morton Thiokel, the rocket manufacturer, communicated to NASA the conclusion that the "temperature data [are] not conclusive on predicting primary O-ring blowby" [43]. The next day Challenger took off, the O-rings failed, and the shuttle exploded, killing the seven people on board.

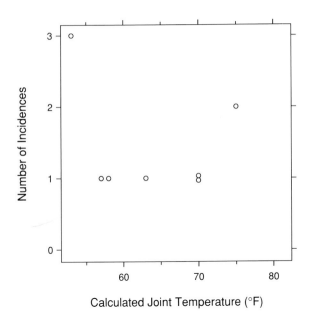

1.4 STATISTICAL REASONING. These data were graphed by space shuttle engineers the evening before the Challenger accident to determine the dependence of O-ring failure on temperature. Data for no failures was not graphed in the mistaken belief that it was irrelevant to the issue of dependence. The engineers concluded from the graph that there is no dependence.

The conclusion of the January 27 analysis was incorrect, in part, because the analysis of the data by the graph in Figure 1.4 was faulty. It omitted data for flights in which no O-rings experienced thermal distress. Figure 1.5 shows a graph with all data included. Now a pattern emerges. The Rogers Commission, a group that intensively studied the Challenger mission afterward, concluded that the engineers had omitted the no-stress data in the mistaken belief that they would contribute no information to the thermal-stress question [43].

Since the densities of different species do not vary radically, we may think of the masses as being surrogate measures for volume, and volume to the 2/3 power behaves like a surface area. Thus the empirical relationship says that brain mass depends on the surface area of the body; Stephen Jay Gould conjectures that this is so because body surfaces serve as end points for so many nerve channels [52]. Now suppose a given species has a greater brain mass than other species with the same body mass; what this means is that

$$(\text{brain mass})/(\text{body mass})^{2/3}$$

is greater. We might expect that the big-brained species would be more intelligent since it has an excess of brain capacity given its body surface. This idea leads to measuring intelligence by this ratio.

Let us now return to Figure 1.6 and consider the graphical problem, which is a serious one. How do we judge the intelligence measure from the graph? Suppose two species have the same intelligence measure; then both have the same value of

$$\frac{(\text{brain mass})}{(\text{body mass})^{2/3}} = r \, .$$

Thus

$$\log(\text{brain mass}) = 2/3 \log(\text{body mass}) + \log(r)$$

for both species. This means that in Figure 1.6, the two equally intelligent species lie on a line with slope 2/3. Suppose one species has a greater value of r than another; then the smarter one lies on a line with slope 2/3 that is to the northwest of the line on which the less intelligent one lies. In other words, to judge the intelligence measure from Figure 1.6 we must mentally superpose a set of parallel lines with slope 2/3. (If we attempt to judge Sagan's mistaken ratios, we must superpose lines with slope 1.) This visual operation is simply too hard.

Figure 1.6 can be greatly improved, at least for the purpose of showing the intelligence measure, by graphing the measure directly on a log scale, as is done in the dot plot of Figure 1.7. Now we can see strikingly many things not so apparent from Figure 1.6. Happily, modern man is at the top. Dolphins are next; interestingly, they are ahead of our ancestor *Homo habilis*.

The problems with Figure 1.6 do not stop here. Five of the labels are wrong. The following are the corrections: "saurornithoid" should be "wolf," "wolf" should be "saurornithoid," "hummingbird" should be "goldfish," "goldfish" should be "mole," and "mole" should be "hummingbird." The correct labels yield the satisfying result that a hummingbird is smaller than a mole.

It should be emphasized that for some purposes, a corrected version of Figure 1.6 is a useful graph. For example, it shows the values of the brain and body masses and gives us information about their relationship. The point is that it does a poor job of showing the intelligence measure.

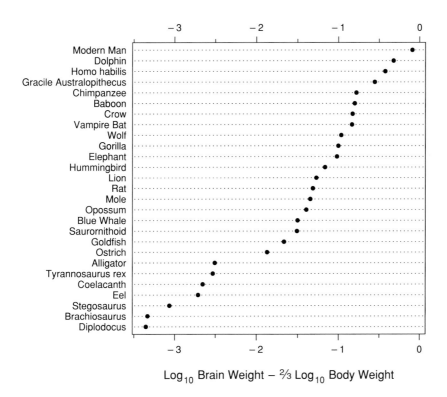

$$Log_{10} \text{ Brain Weight} - \tfrac{2}{3} Log_{10} \text{ Body Weight}$$

1.7 DOT PLOT. The intelligence measure is shown directly by a dot plot. (Both masses are expressed in grams for this computation.) The values of the measure can be judged far more readily than in Figure 1.6. For example, we can see modern man is at the top, even ahead of our very clever fellow mammals, the dolphins. Incorrect labels on Figure 1.6 have been corrected here.

1.3   The Contents of the Book

Chapter 2: Principles of Graph Construction

Figure 1.8 graphs an estimate of average temperature in the Northern Hemisphere following a nuclear war involving 10, 000 megatons of nuclear weapons. The data are from a *Science* article, "Nuclear Winter: Global Consequences of Multiple Nuclear Explosions," by Turco, Toon, Ackerman, Pollack, and Sagan [125]. The temperatures are computed from a series of physical models that describe a script for the nuclear war, for the creation of particles, for radiation production, and for convection. Figure 1.8 shows that the predicted temperature drops to about $-25°C$ and then slowly increases toward the current average ambient temperature in the Northern Hemisphere, which is shown by the horizontal line on the graph.

In Figure 1.8 there are four scale lines that form a rectangle, the tick marks are outside of the rectangle, the size of the rectangle is set so that no values of the data are graphed on top of it, and there are tick marks on all four sides of the graph. Principles of graph construction such as these are the topic of Chapter 2. The focus is on the basic elements: tick marks, scales, captions, plotting symbols, reference lines, keys, and labels. These details of graph construction are critical controlling factors whose proper use can greatly increase the accuracy of the information that we visually decode from displays of data.

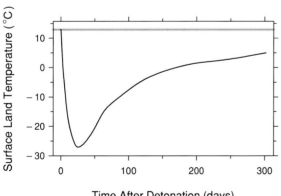

1.8 CHAPTER 2. On this graph there are four scale lines that form a rectangle, the tick marks are outside of the rectangle, the size of the rectangle is set so that no values of the data are graphed on top of it, and there are tick marks on all four sides of the graph. Chapter 2 is about principles of graph construction such as these.

Chapter 3: Graphical Methods

Figure 1.9 is a *dot plot,* a graphical method that was invented to display measurements with labels [23,26]. The large dots convey the values and the dotted lines enable us to visually connect each value with its label. The dot plot has several different forms depending on the nature of the data and the structure of the labels.

The data in Figure 1.9 are the number of speakers for 21 of the world's languages [98]. Only languages spoken by at least 50 million people are shown. The data are graphed on a log base 2 scale, so moving from left to right, values double from one tick mark to the next.

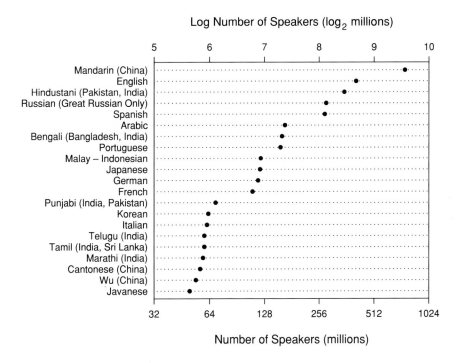

1.9 CHAPTER 3. The figure shows a graphical method called a dot plot, which can be used to show data where each value has a label. The data are the number of speakers for the world's 21 most spoken languages. The data are graphed on a log base 2 scale, so values double in moving left to right from one tick mark to the next.

Figure 1.10 is a graph of ozone against wind speed for 111 days in New York City from May 1 to September 30 of 1973 [13]. The graph shows that ozone tends to decrease as wind speed increases due to the increased ventilation of air pollution that higher wind speeds bring. However, because the pattern is embedded in a lot of noise, it is difficult to see more precise aspects of the pattern, for example, whether there is a linear or nonlinear decrease. In Figure 1.11 a smooth curve has been added to the graph of ozone and wind speed. The curve was computed by a method called *locally weighted regression*, often abbreviated to *lowess*, or *loess* [22,26,28]. Loess provides a graphical summary that helps our assessment of the dependence; now we can see that the dependence of ozone on wind speed is nonlinear. One important property of loess is that it is quite flexible and can do a good job of following a very wide variety of patterns.

Chapter 3 is about graphical methods such as the dot plot, loess, and graphing on a log base 2 scale. Some of the graphs are methods by virtue of the design of the visual vehicle used to convey the data; the dot plot is an example. Other methods use the standard Cartesian graph as the visual vehicle, but are methods by virtue of the quantitative information that is shown on the graph; graphing a loess curve is an example of such a method.

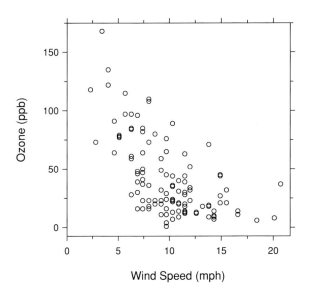

1.10 CHAPTER 3. An air pollutant, ozone, is graphed against wind speed. From the graph we can see that ozone tends to decrease as wind speed increases, but judging whether the pattern is linear or nonlinear is difficult.

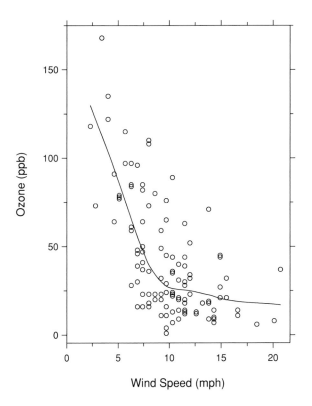

1.11 CHAPTER 3. Loess, a method for smoothing data, is used to compute a curve summarizing the dependence of ozone on wind speed. With the curve superposed, we can now see that the dependence of ozone on wind speed is nonlinear. Chapter 3 is about graphical methods such as loess, dot plots, and graphing on a log base 2 scale.

Chapter 4: Graphical Perception

When a graph is constructed, quantitative and categorical information is *encoded*, chiefly through position, size, symbols, and color. When we study the graph, the information is visually *decoded*. A graphical method is successful only if the decoding process is effective. Informed decisions about how to encode data can be achieved only through an understanding of the visual decoding process, which is called *graphical perception.*

A display method that leads to inefficient visual decoding can prevent important aspects of data from being detected or can lead to distortions in the perception of information. One example was discussed earlier in Section 1.1 (pp. 6–9); the faster rise than fall of the sunspot numbers could not be perceived in the top panel of Figure 1.1.

Figure 1.12 shows another example. The top panel graphs the values of imports and exports between England and the East Indies. The data were first displayed in 1786 by William Playfair [104]. To visually decode the import data we can make judgments of *positions* along the vertical scale; the same is true of exports. Another important set of quantitative values encoded on this graph is the amounts by which imports exceed exports. To visually decode these values we must judge the vertical *distances* between the two curves. But we perform this visual operation inaccurately; our visual system tends to judge minimum distances between two curves rather than vertical distances. For example, from the top panel of Figure 1.12 imports minus exports appear not to change by much during the period just after 1760 when both series are rapidly increasing. This is incorrect. Imports minus exports are graphed directly in the bottom panel of Figure 1.12 so that the values can be visually decoded by judgments of position along a common scale, and now we can see there is a rapid rise and fall just after 1760.

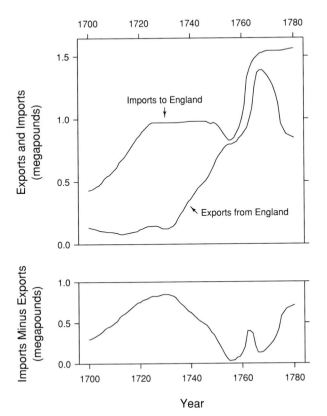

1.12 CHAPTER 4. The top panel is a graph of exports and imports between the East Indies and England. The data are from a graph published by William Playfair in 1786. It is difficult to visually decode imports minus exports, which are encoded by the vertical distances between the curves. Imports minus exports are graphed directly in the bottom panel, and now we can see that their behavior just after 1760 is quite different from what we visually decode in the top panel. Chapter 4 deals with issues of graphical perception such as this.

The only route to an understanding of display methods is rigorous study of graphical perception. Chapter 4 is about such rigorous study. First, a model for graphical perception is presented that provides a framework for investigations of graphical perception. Then the model is used to investigate a number of display methods introduced in earlier chapters. This provides both a justification of the methods and guidance for carrying out other investigations. The rigorous study contrasts with the approach of many past discussions of display methods, where, in medieval-science fashion, pure opinion dominates with no facts to provide guidance.

22

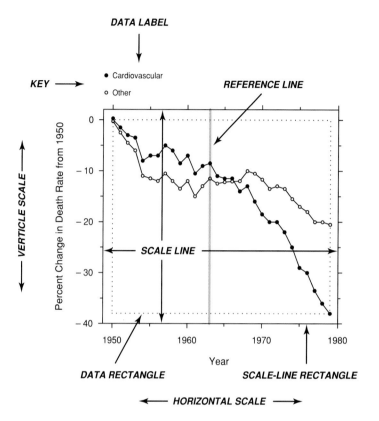

DATA LABEL

KEY →

• Cardiovascular
○ Other

REFERENCE LINE

VERTICLE SCALE

Percent Change in Death Rate from 1950

SCALE LINE

DATA RECTANGLE

Year

SCALE-LINE RECTANGLE

← HORIZONTAL SCALE →

2.1 TERMINOLOGY. This figure and the next define terminology. The two sets of data — death rates due to cardiovascular disease and death rates due to all other diseases — are superposed. The data labels are in the key on this graph.

TITLE

Figure 19. AGE-ADJUSTED DEATH RATE. The data are the percent changes from 1950 in death rate in the United States due to cardivascular disease and other diseases.

CAPTION

2 Principles of Graph Construction

This chapter is about the basic elements of graph construction — scales, captions, plotting symbols, reference lines, keys, labels, panels, and tick marks. Principles of graph construction are given that can enhance the ability of a graph to show the structure of the data. The principles are based on the study of graphical perception, the topic of Chapter 4. They are relevant both for data *analysis*, when the analyst wants to study the data, and for data *communication*, when the analyst wants to present quantitative information to others.

Graphing data is difficult, and without principles of construction problems can occur. The chapter contains many examples of graphs from science and technology that have problems. The principles are applied to the examples to solve the problems.

Section 2.1 (pp. 23–25) defines terms. Section 2.2 (pp. 25–54) gives principles that make the elements of a graph visually clear, and Section 2.3 (pp. 54–66) gives principles that contribute to a clear understanding of what is graphed. Section 2.4 (pp. 66-79) is about the aspect ratio of a graph — its height divided by its width. Section 2.5 (pp. 80–109) is about scales, and Section 2.6 (pp. 110–118) discusses general strategies for graphing data.

2.1 Terminology

Terminology for graphical displays is unfortunately not fully developed and usage is not consistent. Thus, in some cases we will have to invent a few terms and in some other cases we will pick one of several possible terms now in use. Terminology is defined in Figures 2.1 and 2.2, which display the percent changes from 1950 in death rates in the United States due to cardiovascular disease and due to all other diseases [82]. The words in boldface convey the terminology. For the most part, the terms are self-explanatory, but a few comments are in order.

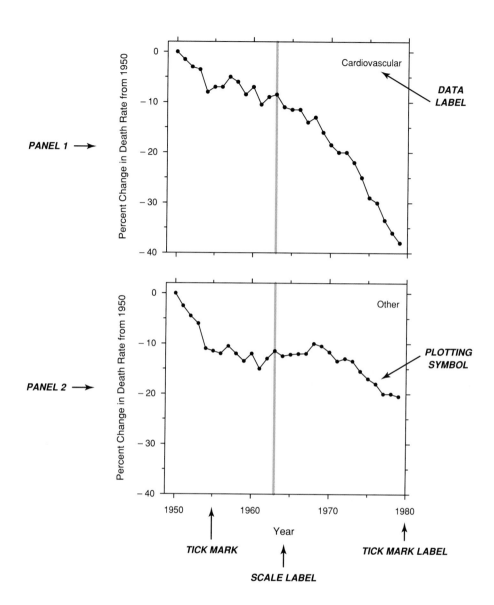

Figure 19. AGE-ADJUSTED DEATH RATE. The data are
the percent changes from 1950 in death rate in the United
States due to cardivascular disease and other diseases.

2.2 TERMINOLOGY. This figure also defines the meaning of terms. The two sets of
data are juxtaposed by using two panels. Each panel on this graph has a data label.

The *scale-line rectangle* is the rectangle formed by the scale lines. The *data rectangle* is the rectangle that just encloses the data. In Figure 2.1 the two data sets are *superposed* and in Figure 2.2 they are *juxtaposed*. The *reference line* shows the time of the first specialized cardiovascular care unit in a hospital in the United States. In Figure 2.1 the *data labels* are part of the *key*, but in Figure 2.2 they are inside the scale-line rectangles.

Scale has two meanings in graphical data display. One is the ruler along which we graph the data; this is the meaning indicated in Figure 2.1. But scale is also used by some to mean the number of data units per cm. This meaning will not be used in this book. Instead, the phrase, *number of units per cm*, will be used. Not every concept needs a single-word definition.

2.2   Clear Vision

Clear vision is a vital aspect of graphing data. The viewer must be able to visually disentangle the many different items that appear on a graph. In this section elementary principles of graph construction are given to help achieve clear vision.

Make the data stand out. Avoid superfluity.

Make the data stand out and *avoid superfluity* are two broad strategies that serve as an overall guide to the specific principles that follow in this section.

The data on a graph are the reason for the existence of the graph. The data should stand out. It is too easy to forget this. There are many ways to obscure the data, such as allowing other elements of the graph to interfere with the data or not making the graphical elements encoding the data visually prominent. Sometimes different values of the data can obscure each other.

We should eliminate superfluity in graphs. Unnecessary parts of a graph add to the clutter and increase the difficulty of making the necessary elements — the data — stand out. Edward R. Tufte puts it aptly; he calls superfluous elements on a graph *chartjunk* [121].

The specific principles that follow in this section will allow us to achieve the two general goals of making the data stand out and avoiding superfluity.

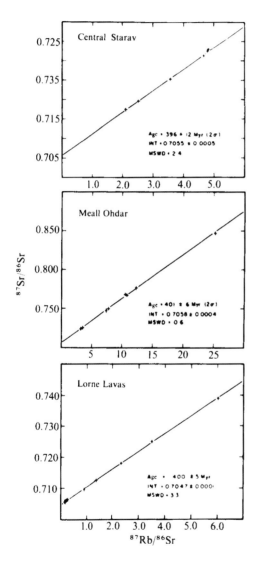

2.5 VISUAL PROMINENCE. The data do not stand out.

Use visually prominent graphical elements to show the data.

On the graph in Figure 2.5 the data do not stand out [20]. The plotting symbols are not visually prominent, and in the bottom panel we cannot tell how many data values make up the black blob in the lower left corner.

A good way to help the data to stand out is to show them with a graphical element that is visually prominent. This is illustrated in Figure 2.6; the data from Figure 2.5 are regraphed. The symbols showing the data stand out, and now the data can be seen. The symbols that look like the spokes of a wheel represent multiple points; each spoke is one point. For example, the spoked symbol in the Lorne Lavas panel represents four data values.

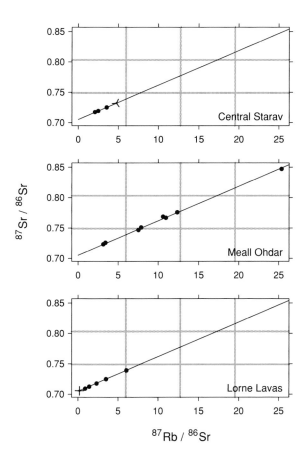

2.6 VISUAL PROMINENCE. *Use visually prominent graphical elements to show the data.* Now the data from Figure 2.5 can be seen. The symbols that look like the spokes of a wheel represent multiple points; each spoke is one observation.

There are other problems with Figure 2.5 that have been corrected in Figure 2.6. First, in the top panel of Figure 2.5, two tick mark labels, 0.725 and 0.735, have been interchanged. Also, it is hard to compare data on the three graphs in Figure 2.5 because the scales are different; scale issues such as these will be discussed in Section 2.5 (pp. 80–109).

When plotting symbols are connected by lines, the symbols should be prominent enough to prevent being obscured by the lines. In Figure 2.7 the data and their standard errors are inconspicuous, in part because of the connecting lines [10].

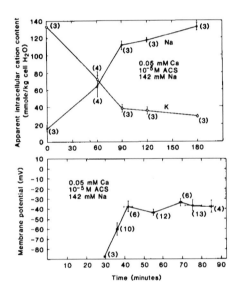

2.7 VISUAL PROMINENCE. The data on this graph do not stand out because the graphical elements showing the observations and their standard errors are not prominent enough to prevent being obscured by the connecting lines.

In Figure 2.8 visually prominent filled circles show the data. These large, bold plotting symbols make the data amply visible and ensure that the connecting of one datum to the next by a straight line does not obscure the data. The connection is useful since it helps us to track visually the movement of the values through time.

The data in Figure 2.8 are from observations of nesting sites of bald eagles in northwestern Ontario [55]. The graph shows good news: in 1973 DDT was banned, and after the ban, the average number of young per site began increasing.

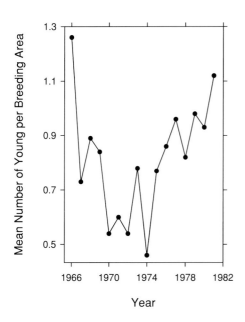

2.8 VISUAL PROMINENCE. The plotting symbols on this graph are prominent enough to prevent being obscured by the connecting lines.

Use a pair of scale lines for each variable. Make the data rectangle slightly smaller than the scale-line rectangle. Tick marks should point outward.

Data are frequently obscured by graphing them on top of scale lines. One example is Figure 2.9 where points are graphed on top of the vertical scale line. The graph and data of Figure 2.9 are from an interesting experiment run by four Harvard anatomists — Charles Lyman, Regina O'Brien, G. Cliett Greene, and Elaine Papafrangos [85]. In the experiment, the researchers observed the lifetimes of 144 Turkish hamsters (*Mesocricetus brandti*) and the percentages of their lifetimes that the hamsters spent hibernating. The goal of the experiment was to determine whether there is an association between the amount of hibernation and the length of life; the hypothesis is that increased hibernation *causes* increased life. Hamsters were chosen for the experiment since they can be raised in the laboratory and since they hibernate for long periods when exposed to the cold. Certain species of bats also hibernate for long periods in the cold but, as the experimenters put it, "their long life-span challenges the middle-aged investigator to see the end of the experiment."

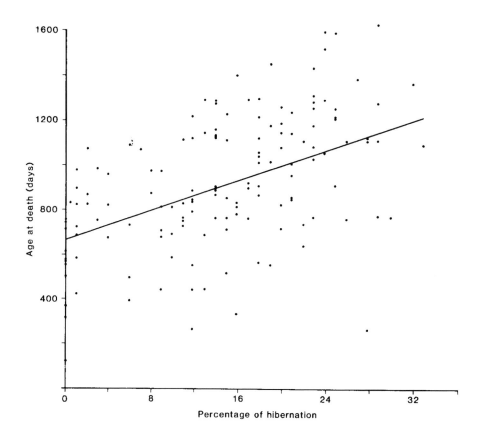

2.9 SCALE LINES AND THE DATA RECTANGLE. The data for zero hibernation are
obscured by the left vertical scale line.

The graph in Figure 2.9 suggests that hibernation and lifetime are
associated; while this does not *prove* causality it does support the
hypothesis. The graph also shows one deviant hamster that spent a large
fraction of its life hibernating but nevertheless died at a young age.
Hibernation cannot save a hamster from all of the perils of life.

One unfortunate aspect of Figure 2.9 is that the data for hamsters with zero hibernation are graphed on top of the vertical scale line. This obscures the data to the point where it is hard to perceive just how many points there are. No data should be so obscured. One way to avoid this is shown in Figure 2.10. The data rectangle is slightly smaller than the scale-line rectangle. Now the values with zero hibernation can be seen clearly.

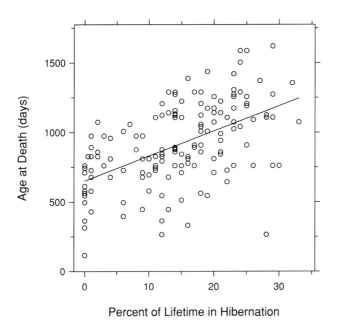

2.10 SCALE LINES AND THE DATA RECTANGLE. *Use a pair of scale lines for each variable. Make the data rectangle slightly smaller than the scale-line rectangle. Tick marks should point outward.* This format prevents data from being obscured. Using two scale lines for each of the two variables on this graph, instead of just one, allows easier table look-up of the scale values of data at the top or right of the data rectangle.

Four scale lines are used in Figure 2.10 rather than the two of Figure 2.9. Table look-up — judging the scale value of a point by judging its position along a scale line — is easier and more accurate as the distance of the point from the scale line decreases. The consequence of one vertical scale line on the left is that the vertical scale values of data to the right are harder to look up than those of data to the left because the rightmost values are further from the line; similarly, when there is just one horizontal scale line, the horizontal scale values of data at the top are harder to look up than those at the bottom. By using four scale lines, the graph treats the data in a more nearly equitable fashion.

Ticks point outward in Figure 2.10 because ticks that point inward can obscure data, as is illustrated in the upper panels of Figure 2.11 [62].

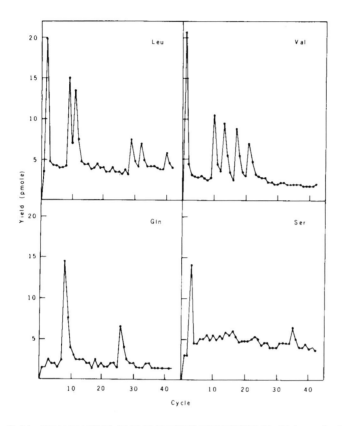

2.11 SCALE LINES AND THE DATA RECTANGLE. Tick marks that point inward can obscure data.

The four scale lines also provide a clearly defined region where our eyes can search for data. With just two, data can be camouflaged by virtue of where they lie. This is true for the data in Figure 2.12 [133]; it is easy to overlook the three points hidden in the upper left corner. In Figure 2.13 the graph has four scale lines and the three points are more prominent.

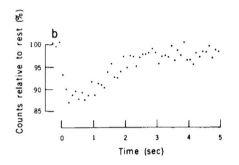

2.12 SCALE LINES AND THE DATA RECTANGLE.
The three points in the upper left are camouflaged.

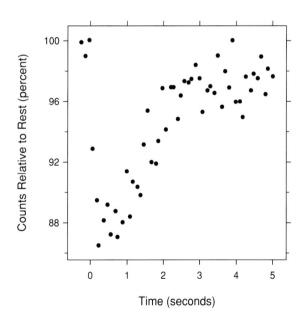

2.13 SCALE LINES AND THE DATA RECTANGLE. The four scale lines provide a clearly defined region for our eyes to look for data. Now, none of the data from Figure 2.12 are in danger of being overlooked.

Figure 2.16 [76] is also cluttered; the error bars interfere with one another so much that it is hard to see the values they portray. One solution is shown in Figure 2.17. In the left three panels the three data sets are juxtaposed and in the right panel they are superposed, but without the error bars. The juxtaposition allows us to see clearly each set of data and its error bars; the superposition allows us to compare the three sets of data more effectively.

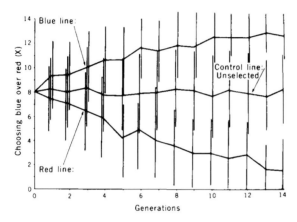

2.16 CLUTTER. This graph is also cluttered.

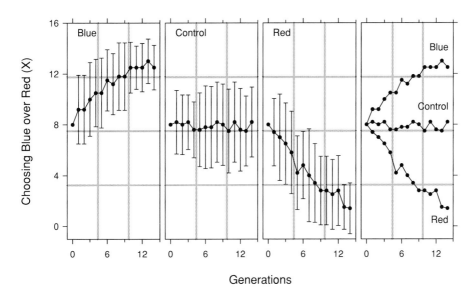

2.17 CLUTTER. The clutter of Figure 2.16 has been eliminated by graphing the data on juxtaposed panels. The right panel is included so that the values of the three data sets can be more effectively compared.

Do not overdo the number of tick marks.

A large number of tick marks is usually superfluous. From 3 to 10 tick marks are generally sufficient; this is just enough to give a broad sense of the measurement scale and to enable sufficiently accurate table look-up. Copious tick marks date back to a time when data were communicated by graphs. Today, we have electronic communication. Every aspect of a graph should serve an important purpose. Any superfluous aspects, such as unneeded tick marks, should be eliminated to decrease visual clutter and thus increase the visual prominence of the most important element — the data.

Figure 2.18, from Carl Sagan's book, *The Dragons of Eden* [107], has too many tick marks. The filled circles show the number of bits of information (horizontal scale) in the DNA of various species when they emerged and the time of their emergence (vertical scale). The open circles show, in the same way, the bits of information in the brains of various species. On a first look at this graph, the bottom scale line makes it easy to think there are two horizontal scales. This is not so. The labels of the form 3×10^k are showing, approximately, the values of the midpoints of the numbers of the form 10^k. For example, midway between 10^7 and 10^8 on a log scale is

$$10^{7.5} = 10^{0.5} \, 10^7 \approx 3 \times 10^7 \, .$$

The large number of tick marks and labels needlessly clutters the graph, and the approximation can easily lead to confusion.

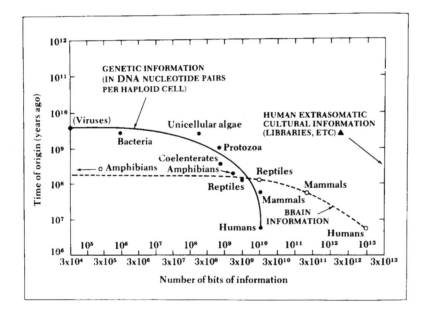

2.18 TICK MARKS. There are too many tick marks and tick mark labels on this graph. The tick mark labels on the horizontal scale are confusing.

In Figure 2.19 the brain and DNA data are graphed again with fewer tick marks and labels; the horizontal and vertical scales have been interchanged so that time is now on the horizontal scale with earlier times on the left and later times on the right.

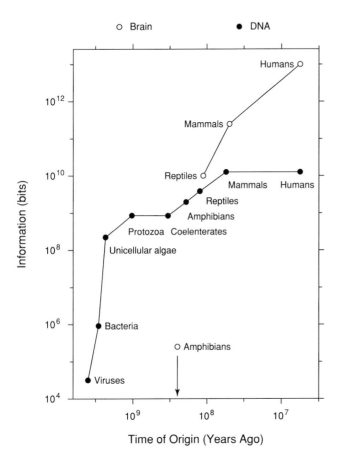

2.19 TICK MARKS. *Do not overdo the number of tick marks.* The vertical scale of this graph, previously the horizontal scale of Figure 2.18, has a sensible number of tick marks and labels.

Use a reference line when there is an important value that must be seen across the entire graph, but do not let the line interfere with the data.

    Reference lines are used in Figure 2.20. The data are the weights of the Hershey Bar, the famous American candy bar. These data, and Stephen Jay Gould's analysis of them [53], are discussed in detail in Section 3.8 (pp. 180–192). The vertical reference lines, which show times of price increases, cross the entire graph and let us see what happened to weight exactly at the times of the price increases. Except for the change from 30 cents to 35 cents, all price increases were accompanied by a size increase.

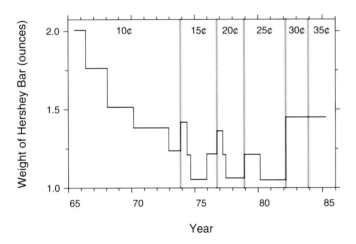

2.20 REFERENCE LINES. *Use a reference line when there is an important value that must be seen across the entire graph, but do not let the line interfere with the data.* The weight of the Hershey Bar is graphed against time. The vertical reference lines divide time up into price epochs; prices are shown just below the top vertical scale. The precision of the reference lines is needed to show us exactly where the price increases occur.

Do not allow data labels in the interior of the scale-line rectangle to interfere with the quantitative data or to clutter the graph.

Figure 2.21 shows the relationship between the average number of bad teeth in 11 and 12 year old children and the per capita sugar consumption per year for 18 countries and the state of Hawaii [97]. When it is important to convey the names for the individual values of a data set, data labels inside of the scale-line rectangle are generally unavoidable. In so doing we should attempt to reduce the visual prominence of the labels so that they interfere as little as possible with our ability to assess the overall pattern of the quantitative data. This has been done in Figure 2.21 by choosing a plotting symbol that is visually very different from the letters of the labels.

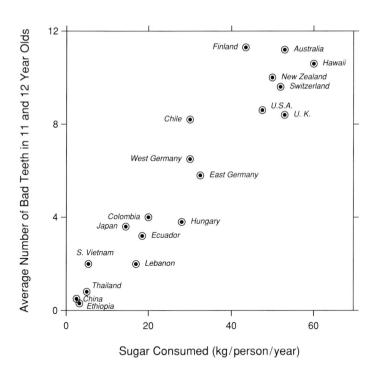

2.21 DATA LABELS. *Do not allow data labels in the interior of the scale-line rectangle to interfere with the quantitative data or to clutter the graph.* The data labels on this graph are needed to convey the names. The visual impact of the labels has been lessened so that they interfere as little as possible with our visual assembly of the plotting symbols.

Sometimes a key is needed to identify data sets, either because data labels inside the scale-line rectangle would add too much clutter or because the values for each data set cannot be identified without using different plotting symbols for the different data sets. A key is used in Figure 2.24 for both reasons. On this graph the data labels are long and the data rectangle is already host to many things. Furthermore, a key is needed because there is no other convenient way to allow identification of the values below $-2 \log_{10}$ (counts/sec), which are shown at the bottom of the graph.

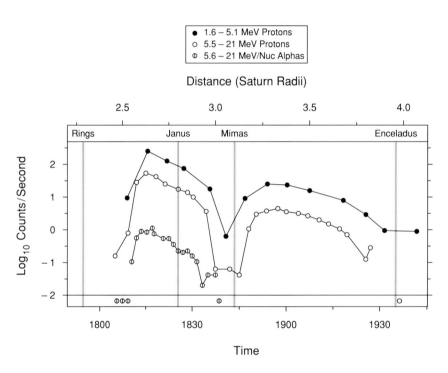

2.24 DATA LABELS. Groups of data values also can be identified by a key. One disadvantage, compared with data labels inside the scale-line rectangle, is that identification is slightly harder because we must look back and forth between the key and the data. However, one advantage over data labels inside, an important one in this example, is that clutter is reduced.

Avoid putting notes and keys inside the scale-line rectangle. Put a key outside, and put notes in the caption or in the text.

We should approach the interior of the scale-line rectangle with a strong spirit of minimalism and try to keep as much out as possible. Not doing so can jeopardize our relentless pursuit of making the data stand out. There is no reason why keys and notes need to appear in the interior.

Keys can go outside of the scale-line rectangle and notes can go in the text or the caption. This has not been done in Figure 2.25 [130] and the result is needless clutter and a confusing graph. The main graph shows release rates of xenon-133 from the Three Mile Island nuclear reactor accident and concentrations of xenon in the air of Albany, N.Y. during

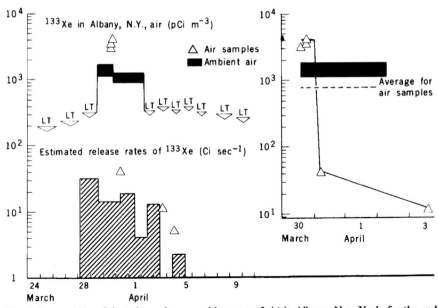

Fig. 1. Xenon-133 activity (picocuries per cubic meter of air) in Albany, New York, for the end of March and early April 1979. The lower trace shows the time-averaged estimates of releases (curies per second) from the Three Mile Island reactor (2). The inset shows detailed values for air samples (gas counting) and concurrent average values for ambient air (Ge diode). Abbreviation: *LT*, less than.

2.25 NOTES AND KEYS. Everything — including the scale labels, a key, and "LT" (meaning less than) — has been thrown into the interior of the scale-line rectangle of this graph. The result is confusing.

the same time period. The purpose of the graph is to show that in Albany, about 500 km from Three Mile Island and downwind during the period of the accident, xenon concentrations rose after the accident.

Figure 2.25 has a number of problems arising from some unusual and unexplained conventions and from putting too much inside the scale-line rectangle. The writing inside is really two scale labels, complete with units. The top label describes two types of Albany air concentration measurements. The bottom label describes the Three Mile Island release rates. Part of the difficulty in comprehending this graph is that three Albany air samples are below the label for release rates, which gives an initial incorrect impression that they are air samples measuring the release rates. The ambient air measurements are shown in a somewhat unconventional way. The two solid rectangles are averages over two intervals; the width shows the averaging interval and a good guess is that the height, which is not explained, shows an average ± 2 sample standard deviations. The triangles with "LT" above them indicate other ambient air measurements which are "less than" the values indicated. The inset has very little additional information; it shows two averages and repeats 5 of the air sample measurements. There is an inaccuracy somewhere; for the three largest air sample values, the times shown on the inset do not agree with the times shown on the main graph. The two averages in the inset do not convey any important information.

These data deserve two panels and deserve less inside the scale-line rectangle to make completely clear what has been graphed. This has been done in Figure 2.26; the writing, key, and LT's have been removed from the scale-line rectangle and the inset has been deleted. The bottom panel shows the release rates of xenon from Three Mile Island; the horizontal line segments show averages over various time intervals. The top panel shows the Albany measurements; the horizontal line segments show intervals over which some measurements were averaged, the error bars show plus and minus two sample standard deviations (if the guess about Figure 2.25 was correct), and an arrow indicates the actual value was less than or equal to the graphed value. Furthermore, the labels for the two types of measurements have been corrected. Both are ambient air measurements and both are from air samples. The terms "continuous monitor" and "grab samples" correctly convey the nature of the two types.

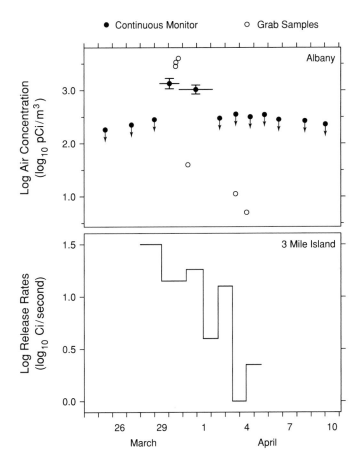

2.26 NOTES AND KEYS. *Avoid putting notes and keys inside the scale-line rectangle. Put a key outside, and put notes in the caption or in the text.* The graph in Figure 2.25 has been improved by the following actions: removing the writing and the key from the interior of the scale-line rectangle; removing the inset altogether; showing the two data sets on separate panels; removing the idiosyncrasies; and correcting the labels describing the two types of measurements.

Overlapping plotting symbols must be visually distinguishable.

Unless special care is taken, overlapping plotting symbols can make it impossible to distinguish individual data points. This happens in several places in Figure 2.27 [18]. The data are from an experiment on the production of mutagens in drinking water. For each category of observation (free chlorine, chloramine, and unchlorinated) there are two observations for each value of water volume. That is, duplicate measurements were made. But two values do not always appear because of exact or near overlap. For example, for the unchlorinated data only one observation appears for water volume just above 0.5 liters.

This problem of visual clarity is a surprisingly tough one. Several solutions are given in Section 3.5 (pp. 154–165).

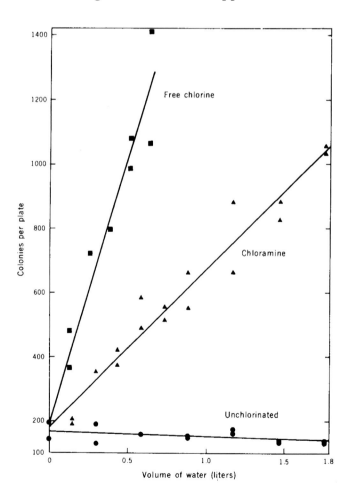

2.27 OVERLAPPING PLOTTING SYMBOLS. *Overlapping plotting symbols must be visually distinguishable.* On this graph, because of exact and near overlap, some of the data cannot be seen.

Superposed data sets must be readily visually assembled.

It is very common for graphs to have two or more data sets superposed within the same data rectangle. We already have encountered many such graphs in this book. Special methods are often required to ensure good visual assembly of each of the different data sets.

In Figure 2.28 [91] it is difficult to visually disentangle the solid squares, circles, and triangles; such plotting symbols are in general visually similar, but in Figure 2.28 the problem is exacerbated by the symbols not being crisply drawn.

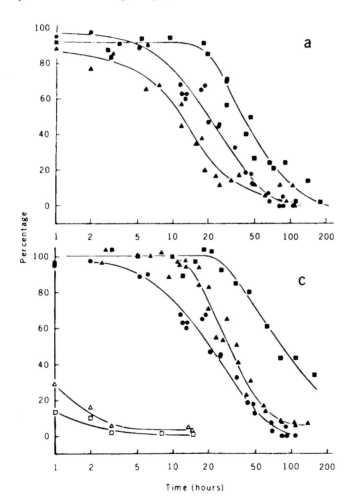

2.28 SUPERPOSED DATA SETS. *Superposed data sets must be readily visually assembled.* On this graph we cannot easily visually assemble the circles as a group, or the squares, or the triangles.

In Figure 2.31 [94] the lines that are supposed to connect the labels with the curves are washed out. Lines, curves, and lettering must be heavy enough and symbols must be large enough to withstand reduction and reproduction.

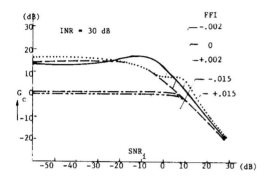

2.31 REDUCTION AND REPRO-
DUCTION. The lines from the curves to
their labels are washed out.

2.3   Clear Understanding

Graphs are powerful tools for communicating quantitative information in written documents. The principles of this section, which are oriented toward the task of communication, contribute to a clear understanding of what is graphed.

Put major conclusions into graphical form. Make captions comprehensive and informative.

Communication of the results of technical studies, when the results involve quantitative issues, can be greatly enhanced by visual displays that speak to the essence of the results. Graphs and their captions can incisively communicate important data and important conclusions drawn from the data. One good approach is to make the sequence of graphs and their captions as nearly independent as possible and to have them summarize evidence and conclusions. This book has been constructed in this way; the graphs and their captions summarize the ideas, and the text has been written around the sequence of graphs. This is to be expected of a book on graphs, but it is also an effective device for other writings in science and technology.

For a graph to be understood clearly, there must be a clear, direct explanation of the data that are graphed and of the inferences drawn from the data. Here is a framework for figure *captions* that can contribute to such a clear explanation:

1. Describe everything that is graphed.

2. Draw attention to the important features of the data.

3. Describe the conclusions that are drawn from the data on the graph.

The framework is illustrated in the caption of Figure 2.32. The data are involved in an astounding discovery that sounds more like science fiction than a highly supportable scientific hypothesis. Sixty-five million years ago extraordinary mass extinctions of a wide variety of animal species occurred, marking the end of the Cretaceous period and the beginning of the Tertiary. The dinosaurs died out along with the marine reptiles and the flying reptiles such as the ichthysaur. Many marine invertebrates also became extinct; ocean plankton almost disappeared completely.

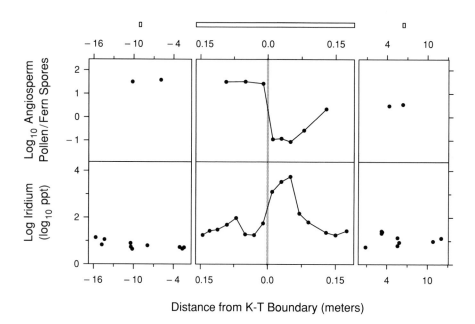

Distance from K-T Boundary (meters)

2.32 EXPLANATION. *Put major conclusions into graphical form. Make captions comprehensive and informative.* Describe everything that is graphed and convey the conclusion drawn from the data. The following is a caption, including the title, that might accompany this graph in its original subject matter context: ANGIOSPERM-FERN RATIO AND IRIDIUM NEAR THE *K–T* BOUNDARY. The graph shows measurements of a core from northeastern New Mexico. The horizontal scale is in meters from the boundary between the Cretaceous and the Tertiary periods; negative values are below the *K–T* boundary so time goes from earlier to later in going from left to right. The widths of the three rectangles at the top of the graph show the same number of meters on the horizontal scales of the three panels. The top panel shows the ratio of angiosperm pollen to fern spores; the *K–T* boundary is taken to be the time point at which these values begin to decrease. The bottom panel shows concentrations of iridium; the concentrations begin a dramatic rise and fall at the boundary. Since the principal source of iridium is extraterrestrial, its rise and fall supports the hypothesis that an asteroid struck the earth causing a cloud of dust in the upper atmosphere; this is argued to have caused the large number of extinctions, including the dinosaurs, that occurred at the beginning of the Tertiary period.

What could have caused such a calamity? Luis Alvarez, Walter Alvarez, Frank Asaro, and Helen Michel at Berkeley made a fortuitous discovery that suggested a cause. They found unusually high levels of iridium right at the K-T (Cretaceous-Tertiary) boundary in sediments from Italy, Denmark, and New Zealand [2]. It is likely that the high iridium levels have an extraterrestrial cause; asteroids and meteors are rich in iridium while the earth's crust is not because this heavy element sank to the core during the earth's molten years. From these data and other information, the four hypothesized that an asteroid, 10 ± 4 km in diameter, struck the earth and sent a dust cloud into the atmosphere that blocked sunlight for a period of several months or even years. The loss of light interfered with food chains and led to the mass extinctions. As the dust from the asteroid settled it deposited an iridium-rich layer on the surface of the earth.

The asteroid hypothesis has been supported by subsequent measurements. Among them are measurements of pollen, fern spores, and iridium in New Mexico [100]. These are the data shown in Figure 2.32. The horizontal scale is distance in the sediment from the K-T boundary. Distance, of course, is just a surrogate for time, which goes from earlier to later as we go from left to right. The top panel graphs the logarithm of the ratio of pollen to fern spores. The point at which the ratio begins to decrease is taken to be the K-T boundary because at the beginning of the Tertiary period angiosperms declined relative to ferns. Just after this boundary there is a peak in the iridium concentrations, shown in the bottom panel.

The caption of Figure 2.32 follows the three-step guidelines presented earlier. The graph and its caption can nearly stand alone as a document that conveys the basic idea of the asteroid-impact hypothesis and the quantitative information that gives it credence.

The interplay between graph, caption, and text is a delicate one that requires substantial judgment. No complete prescription can be designed to allow us to proceed mechanically and to relieve us of thinking hard. However, a viewer is usually well served by a caption that makes a graph as self-contained as possible. If there are several graphs, the captions collectively can be an independent piece; for example, a detailed description of a data set described in one graph caption does not need to be repeated in a subsequent graph caption.

It is possible, though, to overdo a comprehensive caption. Putting a description of the experimental procedure in the caption seems to go too far. It burdens the graph and makes what should be a concise summary into a tome. Figure 2.33 [133] is an example. The ratio of caption area to graph area is 2.8; this is too much detail. The details of an experimental procedure must be communicated, but surely there is a better place than a figure caption, which is a summary.

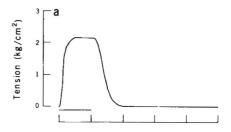

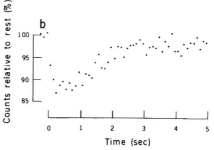

Fig. 2. Tension and the intensity of the 42.9-nm layer line during 1-second tetanus at the sarcomere length of 2.2 μm. (a) Tension record averaged over the 40 tetanic contractions required for obtaining the time course of the layer-line intensity. A sartorius muscle was dissected from *Rana catesbeiana* and tetanized for 1 second at 2-minute intervals. The horizontal line represents the period of stimulation. Tension was recorded with an isometric tension transducer (Shinkoh, type UL). (b) Intensity of the first-order myosin layer line at 42.9 nm. The x-ray source was a rotating-anode generator (Rigaku FR) with a fine focus (1.0 by 0.1 mm) on a copper target. This was operated at 50 kV with a tube current of 70 mA; such a high power was possible with an anode of a large diameter (30 cm) rotating at a high speed (9000 rev/min). A bent-crystal monochromator was used at a source-to-crystal distance of 25 cm with a viewing angle of 6°. The intensity of the myosin layer line was measured with a scintillation counter combined with a mask; the mask had apertures at the positions of the off-meridional parts of the first-order layer line. The meridional reflection at 14.3 nm is known to be slightly displaced during contraction, suggesting a minute change in the myosin periodicity (*1, 3*). It is, therefore, possible that the 42.9-nm layer line is also slightly displaced. However, the possible displacement (14 μm at the position of the mask) would be insignificant compared with the width of each aperture (0.8 mm). The intensity measured at the resting state was 1400 count/sec. The intensities during and after tetanus were expressed as percentages of the resting intensity and plotted against time after the first stimulus of each set of stimuli. Each point represents the intensity averaged over a 100-msec period. The first three points represent the measurements made before stimulation.

2.33 EXPLANATION. It is possible to overdo the explanation in a caption. The complete description of the experimental procedure in this caption is too much detail. The ratio of the caption area to the graph area is 2.8.

Too little detail, however, occurs more frequently in graphs in science and technology than too much detail. Figure 2.34 [40] is an example. The bars and error bars are not explained anywhere. One good guess is that they are sample means and estimates of the standard errors of the means; guessing should not be necessary.

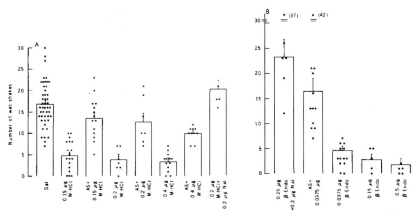

Fig. 1. Inhibitory effect of morphine hydrochloride (A) and β-endorphin (B) on wet-shake behavior in rats. Antagonism was by antibody to cerebroside sulfate (AS). A volume of 2 μl was delivered into the PAG in 1-μl increments with a 1-minute interval in between. The control consisted of saline (Sal). Morphine HCl (M-HCl) and β-endorphin were preceded by saline, AS, or naloxone (Nal) as indicated. The dose of morphine HCl and naloxone refers to the chloride salt. Each point is the datum for one animal. The AS + morphine HCl groups are all significantly different (t-test, P < .005) from the corresponding morphine HCl groups alone (A). The group receiving AS + 0.0375 μg of β-endorphin is also significantly different (P < .005) from the group receiving 0.0375 μg of β-endorphin (B).

2.34 EXPLANATION. The more common problem of scientific data display is too little explanation, rather than too much. The bars and error bars on this graph are not explained in the text or in the caption.

Error bars should be clearly explained.

Error bars are a convenient way to convey variability in data. Unfortunately, terminology is so inconsistent in science and technology that it is easy for an author to say one thing and a viewer to understand something else. Error bars can convey one of several possibilities:

(1) The *sample standard deviation* of the data.

(2) An *estimate of the standard deviation* (also called the *standard error*) of a statistical quantity.

(3) A *confidence interval* for a statistical quantity.

As an example, let us consider a particular case, also the most frequent one. Suppose the data are $x_1, \ldots, x_n$ and the statistical quantity being graphed is the sample mean,

$$\overline{x} = \frac{1}{n} \sum_{i=1}^{n} x_i \, .$$

The sample standard deviation of the data is

$$s = \sqrt{\frac{1}{(n-1)} \sum_{i=1}^{n} (x_i - \overline{x})^2} \, .$$

An estimate of the standard error of the mean is

$$s/\sqrt{n} \, .$$

If the data are from a normal distribution then a 95% confidence interval for the population mean is $(\overline{x} - k\, s/\sqrt{n}, \, \overline{x} + k\, s/\sqrt{n})$, where k is a value that depends on n; if n is larger than about 60, k is approximately 1.96.

Error bars are used in Figure 2.35 [64]. In the last sentence of the figure caption we are told that the graphed values "represent means of three to four mice $\pm$ the standard deviation." What are we being shown? Is it (1) or (2) above? It is probably (1), but we should not have to deal with probability in understanding what is graphed.

Error bars should be unambiguously described. For the three cases cited above, the following is some terminology that can prevent ambiguity:

(1) The error bars show plus and minus one sample standard deviation of the data.

(2) The error bars show plus and minus an estimate of the standard deviation (or one standard error) of the statistic that is graphed.

(3) The error bars show a confidence interval for the statistic that is graphed.

Unambiguous description is only one issue with which we need to concern ourselves in showing error bars on graphs. A second important issue is whether they convey anything meaningful. This statistical issue is discussed in Section 3.14 (pp. 212–220).

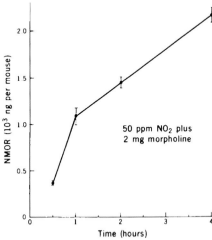

Fig. 1. Time course of NMOR biosynthesis in mice. Groups of three to four male ICR mice were gavaged with freshly prepared solutions of 2 mg of MOR (Aldrich Chemical) in 0.2 ml of distilled water and immediately placed in exposure chambers (Nalge desiccators, modified for gas inflow from the bottom and exhaust from the top). Mice were then exposed to 50 ppm of NO_2 (three to four mice per chamber, 5 cubic feet per hour, 20 volume changes per hour) at intervals of from 0.5 to 4 hours. The required concentrations of NO_2 were produced by mixing stock NO_2 (custom grade, Union Carbide) with air at an appropriate flow rate, prior to introduction into the chambers; we checked the accuracy of the exposure mixtures by periodically monitoring and analyzing the NO_2 in the exhaust from the chambers, using the Griess-Saltzman reaction (19). Concurrent controls consisted of two mice exposed in separate chambers to NO_2 alone for 4 hours, additional controls were gavaged with 2 mg of MOR or 0.2 ml of distilled water and exposed to air for identical periods in separate chambers. After exposure to NO_2, the mice were killed by freezing in liquid nitrogen and blended to a fine powder (20). Two or three aliquots (approximately 8 g each) were taken from each mouse powder and blended with 75 ml of ice-cold 35 percent aqueous methanol in a Waring Blendor (5 minutes, medium speed); a known amount of a nitrosamine standard [152 ng of di-*n*-propylnitrosamine (DPN), Aldrich] was then added, and blending continued for 1 to 2 minutes. Homogenates were divided in half and centrifuged (5000*g*, 25 minutes, 5°C; swinging bucket), supernatant was removed, and the pellets were extracted again with cold 35 percent methanol. The pooled supernates were extracted (twice) with an equal volume (total, 150 ml) of dichloromethane [(DCM), Burdick and Jackson] (21), and the organic layer was dried by passage through a cotton gauze (Ex-tube, Analytichem International) and concentrated to 2 ml in a Kuderna Danish concentrator (Kontes, 250 ml) kept in a 65°C bath. Aliquots (20 *μ*l) of the concentrates from each of two or three powder samples were injected into the thermal energy analyzer–gas chromatograph (Thermo Electron modified model TEA-502) (22) for NMOR analysis. Peaks were identified and quantitated by comparison with the retention time and response of reference nitrosamines (23). The plotted values are corrected for any background control NMOR levels and for the DPN standard recoveries and represent means of three to four mice ± the standard deviation.

2.35 ERROR BARS. *Error bars should be clearly explained.* It is important to distinguish between the sample standard deviation and an estimate of the standard deviation of the sample mean (the standard error of the mean). It is not clear from the explanation of this graph which of these two deviations the error bars portray.

When logarithms of a variable are graphed, the scale label should correspond to the tick mark labels.

The dot plot in Figure 2.36 shows death rates for the leading causes of death of people in the age group 15 to 24 years in the United States [95]. The logarithms of the data are graphed; that is, equal increments on the horizontal scale indicate equal increments of the logarithm of death rate. On the top horizontal scale line the tick mark labels show the values of the data on the original scale; the scale label describes the variable and its units on the original scale, to correspond to the tick mark labels. On the bottom horizontal scale line, the tick mark labels are in log units; the scale label describes the variable and its units on the log scale.

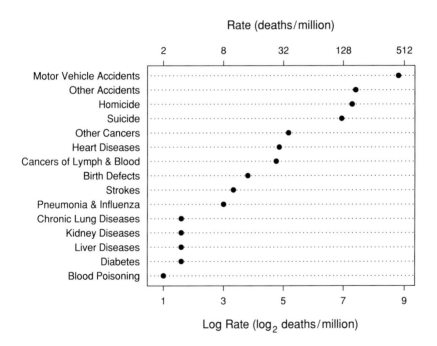

2.36 LABELS FOR LOGS. *When logarithms of a variable are graphed, the scale label should correspond to the tick mark labels.* The logarithms of the data are graphed on this dot plot. On the top horizontal scale line the tick mark labels are in the units of the data on the original scale, so the scale labels describe the data on the original scale. On the lower scale line the tick mark labels are expressed in log units of the data, so the scale label describes the logarithms of the data.

Proofread graphs.

Graphs should be proofread and carefully checked for errors.
Figure 2.37, a graph of measurements of Saturn's magnetic field made by
the Pioneer II spacecraft, has an error; the exponents for the tick mark
labels on the vertical scale line are missing [110]. This is quite
unfortunate since the magnitude of the magnetic field is of much
interest. The authors write about the graph: "This is shown in
Figure 1.1, which presents an overview of the encounter as evident in
the magnitude of the ambient magnetic field." It is unfortunate to have a
graph error degrade the communication of such exciting, high-quality
scientific work.

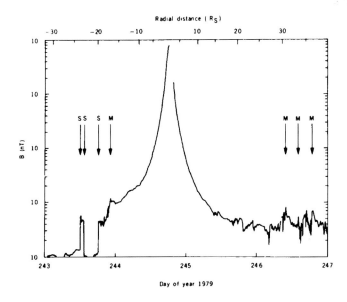

2.37 PROOFREAD. *Proofread graphs.* Graphs should be proofread, just as we do text. On this graph, lack of careful proofreading resulted in missing exponents on the tick mark labels of the vertical scale.

Strive for clarity.

Strive for clarity is really a summation of the principles presented so far; in Section 2.2 (pp. 25–54) the principles contribute to making a graph visually clear, and in this section the principles contribute to a clear understanding of what is graphed. Striving for clarity should be done consciously. We should ask of every graph, "Are the data portrayed clearly?" and "Are the elements of the graph clearly explained?" Let us consider one example.

The data in Figure 2.38 [129] are percentages of degrees awarded to women in several disciplines of science and technology during three time periods. The elements of the graph are not fully explained; little is said in the text, so we must rely on the labeling and the caption to understand what is graphed. At first glance the labels suggest the graph is a standard divided bar chart with the length of the bottom division of each bar showing the percentage for doctorates, the length of the middle division showing the percentage for master's, and the top division showing the bachelor's. This is not so. It would imply that in most cases the percentage of bachelor's degrees given to women is generally lower than the percentage of doctorates.

A little detective work reveals that the three values of the data for each discipline during each time period are determined by the three adjacent, vertical, dashed lines. The top end of the left line indicates the position of the value for doctorates, the middle line indicates the master's degrees, and the right line indicates the bachelor's degrees; the thick horizontal line segments are drawn at the ends of the vertical lines. The horizontal segments are what one sees most prominently, but without intensive visual scrutiny of the graph, it is not possible to determine the degree associated with a particular segment.

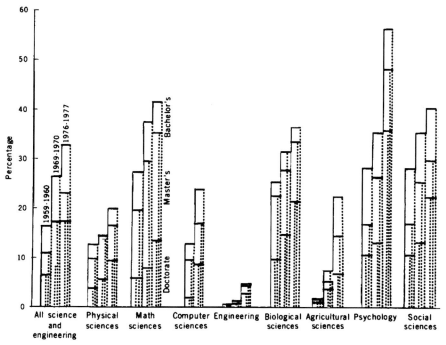

Fig. 1. Proportion of degrees in science and engineering earned by women in 1959 to 1960, 1969 to 1970, and 1976 to 1977 (6). Included in the social science degrees are anthropology, sociology, economics, and political science.

2.38 CLARITY. This graph fails both in clarity of vision and clarity of explanation.

There are other problems with this graph. Only two bars are shown for computer science, with no explanation. One can only assume that the 1959-1960 time period is missing. There is a construction error; the horizontal line for doctorates in all science and engineering in 1969-1970 is missing. Another difficulty with the graph is visual; the bar chart format makes it hard to visually connect the three values of a particular degree for a particular discipline to see change through time.

In Figure 2.39 the data from Figure 2.38 are regraphed. There has been a striving for clarity. It is clear how the data are represented, and the design allows us to see easily the values of a particular degree for a particular discipline through time. Finally, the figure caption explains the graph in a comprehensive and clear way.

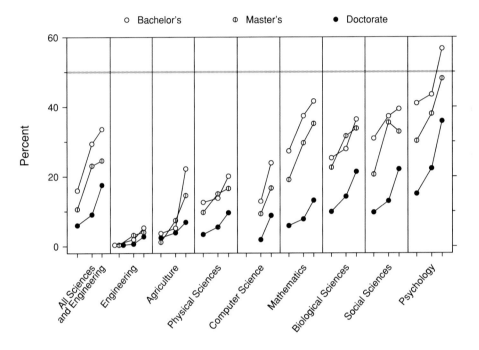

2.39 CLARITY. *Strive for clarity.* This graphing of the data from Figure 2.38 strives for clarity. It shows the percentage of degrees earned by women for three degrees, three time periods, and nine disciplines. For each discipline, the three tick marks indicate the years 1959–1960, 1969–1970, 1976–1977.

2.4 Banking to 45°

The *data rectangle*, defined at the beginning of this chapter, just encloses the data. In Figure 2.40 the same data are graphed twice. On each panel the dotted rectangle is the data rectangle; the shapes of the two rectangles are different because the vertical scale line is shorter in the bottom panel.

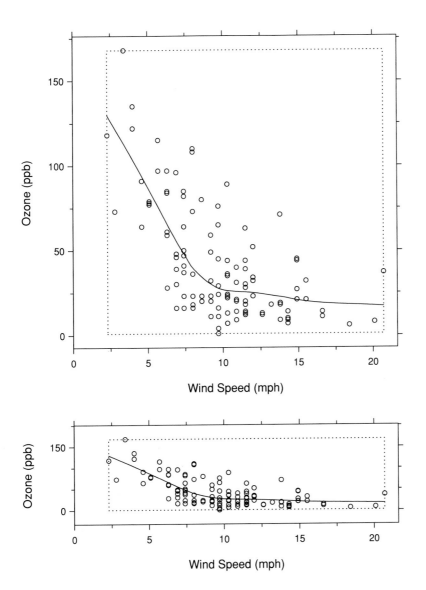

2.40 ASPECT RATIO. The dotted rectangle that just encloses the data on each panel is the data rectangle. The aspect ratio is the height of the data rectangle divided by the width. In the top panel, the aspect ratio is 1 vcm/hcm, and in the bottom panel, it is 0.25 vcm/hcm.

   The *aspect ratio* of a graph is the height of the data rectangle divided by the width. In the top panel of Figure 2.40 the aspect ratio is 1 vcm/hcm, where vcm means vertical centimeters and hcm means horizontal centimeters, and in the bottom panel it is 0.25 vcm/hcm.

The two panels of Figure 2.40 graph the air pollutant ozone against wind speed for 111 days in New York City from May 1 to September 30 of one year [13]. Superposed on each panel is a smooth curve that describes the dependence of ozone on wind speed. For example, we can see that the general pattern is for ozone to decrease as wind speed increases because of the increased ventilation of air pollution that higher wind speeds bring. At each value of wind speed the curve has a slope that encodes the rate of change of ozone as a function of wind speed. The units of this rate of change are ppb/mph. For low values of wind speed, the slope is very negative; in other words, a small increment in wind speed brings a large reduction in ozone. For high values of wind speed, the slope is close to zero; in other words, a small increment in wind speed brings a small reduction in ozone.

Each curve in Figure 2.40 consists of a collection of short connected line segments, the *local line segments*. We visually decode the information about the relative local rate of change of ozone with wind speed by judging the *orientations* of these local segments. The orientation of a segment is its angle with the horizontal. Segments with positive slopes have positive orientations and segments with negative slopes have negative orientations. A segment with slope 1 has an orientation of $45°$, a segment of slope -1 has an orientation of $-45°$, and a segment with zero slope has an orientation of $0°$. The orientations of line segments on a graph change if the aspect ratio of the graph changes. If the aspect ratio increases, there is an increase in the steepness of the orientation of any segment that has a slope other than zero. For example, in the top panel of Figure 2.40, each nonzero orientation is steeper than its counterpart in the bottom panel because the aspect ratio is greater in the top panel.

The aspect ratio of a graph is an important factor for judging rate of change.

The aspect ratio of a display such as Figure 2.40 greatly affects the accuracy of our visual decoding of the rate of change of y with x; as we just saw, the aspect ratio controls the overall steepness of the orientations of line segments, and it is such orientations that we judge to decode information about rate of change. This effect of the aspect ratio is demonstrated in Figure 2.41. The display, discussed previously in Chapter 1, graphs the yearly sunspot numbers from 1749 to 1924. In the top panel, the shape parameter is 1 vcm/hcm, and in the bottom panel, it is 0.055 vcm/hcm. The dominant frequency component of variation of the data is the cycles whose average period is about 11 years. These cycles are evident in both panels of the figure, but the top panel fails to reveal an important property — the cycles rise more rapidly than they fall. The faster rise than fall is most pronounced for the cycles with high peaks, is less pronounced for those with medium peaks, and disappears for those cycles with the very lowest peaks.

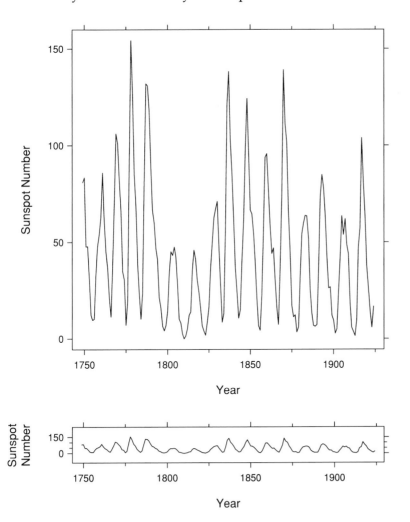

2.41 BANKING. *The aspect ratio of a graph is an important factor for judging rate of change.* The sunspot numbers are graphed in both panels. The aspect ratio is 1 vcm/hcm in the top panel. In the bottom panel the aspect ratio is 0.055 vcm/hcm; the line segments are banked to 45°, which allows us to more accurately visually decode information about rate of change.

The importance of the aspect ratio was recognized as early as 1914 [12], and for many decades there was much discussion. But no one attempted to base discussion on a rigorous investigation of the effect of the aspect ratio on our visual decoding of information. There was no science. The result was numerous, contradictory opinions [33]. This is not surprising since with no facts arising from either convincing theoretical arguments or careful experiments, there was no scientific body of material around which opinions could coalesce.

In the late 1980s the problem was finally attacked using mathematics, the theory of visual perception, and controlled experiments, and the solution was found [25, 33]. Here, we will simply present the results, but in Section 4.7 (pp. 251–256) the scientific enquiry that led to the solution is described.

When the orientations of line segments are judged to decode information about rate of change, bank the segments to 45°.

The judgments of the orientations of line segments are optimized when the aspect ratio is chosen so that the absolute values of the orientations of the segments are centered on 45°. This tends to center the segments with positive slopes on 45° and the segments with negative slopes on −45°. This centering is called *banking to 45°*, a display method whose name suggests the banking of a road to affect its slope. In Section 4.7 (pp. 251–256) a formula is given for the aspect ratio that achieves such banking.

In the bottom panel of Figure 2.41 the local line segments that make up the curve are banked to 45°; the aspect ratio is 0.055 hcm/vcm. It is this banking that allows us to see the faster rise than fall of the sunspots. In the top panel the aspect ratio is 1.00 vcm/hcm; the absolute orientations are centered on an angle much greater than 45°, which degrades the accuracy of our visual decoding of rate of change.

Banking to 45° is used in the top panel of Figure 2.42; the aspect ratio is 1.00 vcm/hcm. The data are a trend curve for atmospheric CO_2 concentrations at Mauna Loa Observatory in Hawaii; the curve was graphed earlier in one panel of Figure 1.2. Through our judgment of the orientations of the banked, local line segments, we see that the curve is convex; this means that the rate of increase of CO_2 is increasing through time. In the bottom panel of Figure 2.42 the aspect ratio is 0.055 vcm/hcm, the optimum value for the sunspot data. But for the CO_2 data, this aspect ratio centers the absolute orientations on an angle much less than 45°; the result is a less accurate perception of rate of change.

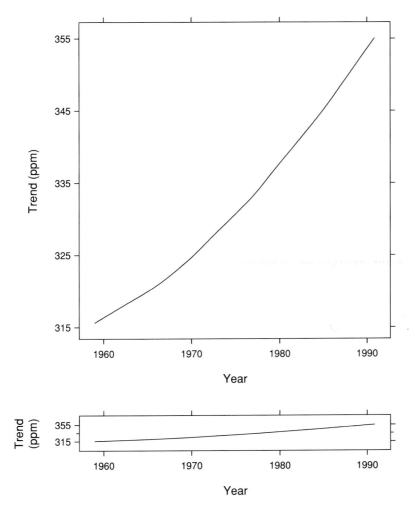

2.42 BANKING. *When the orientations of line segments are judged to decode information about rate of change, bank the segments to 45°.* The CO_2 trend curve is graphed in both panels. In the top panel, the segments are banked to 45° and the aspect ratio is 1.00 vcm/hcm; we can readily judge the convexity of the curve. In the bottom panel, the aspect ratio is 0.055 vcm/hcm; the absolute orientations are centered on an angle much less than 45°, which interferes with our judgment of rate of change.

The principle of banking to 45° is a universal one and applies to the judgment of orientation of any collection of line segments, not just a single curve by itself on a graph as in Figures 2.41 and 2.42. For example, it applies to a curve superposed on a set of points. This is illustrated in Figure 2.43, which graphs the ozone and wind speed data from Figure 2.40. The local segments of the curve are banked to 45°.

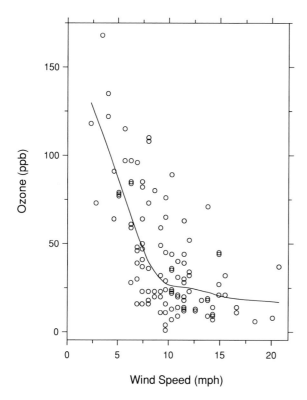

2.43 BANKING. The segments that make up the smooth curve are banked to 45°.

The principle applies to the judgment of orientations of segments on juxtaposed panels with the same scales. This is illustrated in Figure 2.44, shown earlier in Section 2.2 (pp. 25–54). The collection of 84 segments that connect the measurements on the four panels is banked to 45°. There is a simple way to think of this banking. Suppose the data were graphed on a single panel. There would be a single data rectangle, and we would choose the aspect ratio to bank the collection of segments to 45°. For the multipanel display, the scales are exactly the same as they would be on the single-panel display. In other words, for the multipanel display we make four copies of the scale-line rectangle of the single-panel display, and then graph part of the data on each panel.

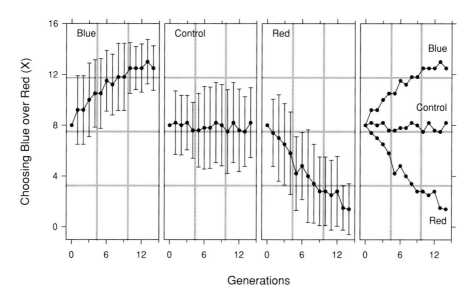

2.44 BANKING. The entire collection of line segments connecting plotting symbols is banked to 45°.

Banking is critical to seeing important effects in Figure 2.45. The data, collected by Bob Milek [93], are from a handgun experiment to study how cartridge velocity, the response, depends on barrel length, the factor. For each handgun, the average cartridge velocity for the first 12 feet from the muzzle was measured for each of several different barrel lengths. On the graph, velocity is graphed against length for nine handguns. One handgun, .223 REM, appears twice with two different types of ammunition. The segments connecting successive values of all of the handgun curves are collectively banked to 45°.

The ability to effectively judge rate of change in Figure 2.45 allows us to see important patterns in the data. First, the overall slopes of the handgun curves tend to increase as we go from bottom to top on the graph. In other words, the increase in velocity as a function of barrel length tends to be greater for handguns with fast cartridges than for those with slow ones. For example, the .223 REM handguns at the top of Figure 2.45 have a much greater rate of increase than the .38 SPL and the .22 LR at the bottom. Second, the underlying pattern in the data for each handgun tends to be concave. In other words, the rate of change of velocity as a function of barrel length tends to decrease as the length increases.

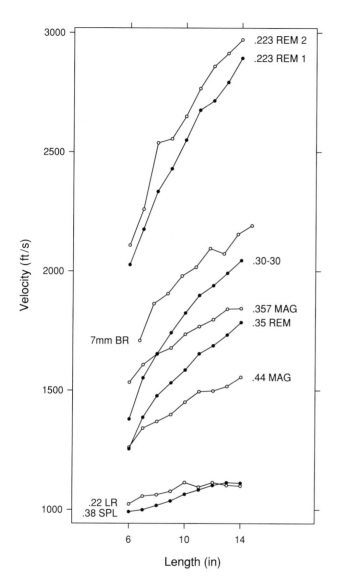

2.45 BANKING. The line segments that connect successive observations are banked to 45°. This allows us to readily perceive that the slopes of the underlying patterns increase as the overall velocity levels increase.

The large variation in the overall slopes for the different handguns, together with the curvature of the patterns, makes the characterization of the data complicated. Transformation of the data, which means new measurement units, might yield more stability in the overall slope and remove or reduce the curvature. It is tempting to try the inverse transformation. This means y is replaced by $1/y$ and x is replaced by $1/x$. The old response was the average velocity of the cartridge over the distance of 12 feet, with units of ft/sec. The new one is the time of travel of the cartridge, with units of msec/ft. The old factor was barrel length, with units of inches. The new one is inverse barrel length, with units of 1/inches. Figure 2.46 graphs the new response against the new factor. Again, the connecting segments are banked to $45°$. The transformations have simplified the patterns. First, the curvature has nearly been removed; the underlying pattern for each handgun is nearly linear except possibly that for the .38 SPL. Second, while the overall slopes appear to vary somewhat, the variation has been substantially reduced.

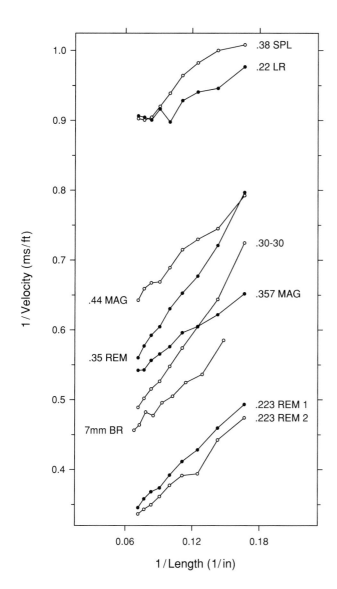

2.46 BANKING. The segments that connect successive observations are banked to 45°. The graph shows that the slopes of the patterns do not depend on the levels.

Suppose v denotes velocity and l denotes barrel length. Figure 2.46 shows that for each handgun,

$$v^{-1} = \alpha + \beta l^{-1},$$

where α and β depend on the characteristics of each handgun, and thus vary from one handgun to the next. Values of α and β were estimated for each handgun by fitting lines to the transformed data using least-squares. The fitted lines are graphed in Figure 2.47 and are banked to 45°.

The display of the velocity data using banking has led to an empirical law for the relationship of v and l. The law stipulates that v depends nonlinearly on l through the mathematical equation

$$v = \frac{l}{\alpha l + \beta} .$$

The equation now allows the derivation of properties of the relationship. For example, Milek, the experimenter, was keen to determine the sensitivity of velocity to an increase in barrel length. The derivative of v with respect to l, which measures the rate of change of v with l, is

$$\frac{dv}{dl} = \frac{\beta}{(\alpha l + \beta)^2} .$$

Thus the derivative decreases monotonically, which means the sensitivity of velocity to length decreases monotonically as the length increases.

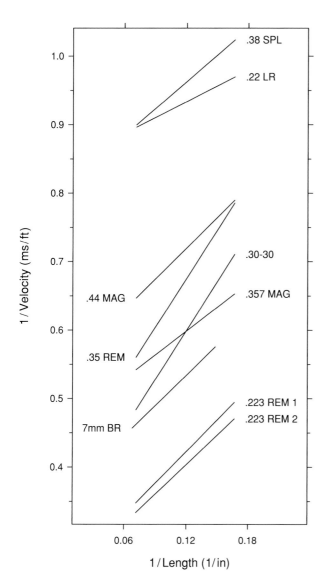

2.47 BANKING. The line segments, which show the least-squares lines fitted to the data, are banked to 45°.

2.5   *Scales*

Scales are fundamental. A graph is a graph, in part, because it has one or more scales. Graphing data would be far simpler if these basic, defining elements of graphs were straightforward, but they are not; scale issues are subtle and difficult.

Choose the range of the tick marks to include or nearly include the range of the data.

The interval from the minimum to the maximum of a set of values is the range of the values. It is a good idea to have the range of the data on a graph be included or nearly included in the range of the tick marks to allow an effective assessment of all of the data. In Figure 2.48 the range of the data on the horizontal scale is included in the range of the tick marks, and the data on the vertical scale are nearly included in the range.

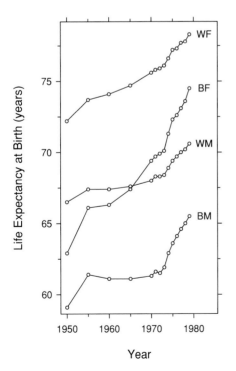

2.48 RANGES. *Choose the range of the tick marks to include or nearly include the range of the data.* The range of the data on the vertical scale is nearly contained within the range of the tick marks. On the horizontal scale the range of the data is completely contained within the range of the tick marks. The line segments connecting successive plotting symbols are banked to 45°.

Subject to the constraints that scales have, choose the scales so that the data rectangle fills up as much of the scale-line rectangle as possible.

There are a number of constraints that affect the choice of scales on graphs. One, just discussed, is that the range of the tick marks should encompass or nearly encompass the range of the data. Another is that we do not want data to be graphed on scale lines. Also, in some cases we want a particular value to be included in the scale; the most common example is showing a zero value. (More will be said later about including zero.) Finally, when different panels of a graph are compared, we will often want the scales to be the same on all panels.

But subject to these constraints, we should attempt to use as much of the interior of the scale-line rectangle as possible. In other words, the data rectangle should lie slightly inside the scale-line rectangle. This is not done in Figure 2.49 [116]. Only 26% of the vertical scale is taken up by the data. Space is wasted on this graph.

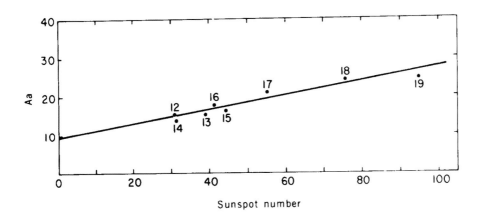

2.49 FILLING THE SCALE-LINE RECTANGLE. Only 26% of the vertical scale is used by the data.

In contrast, Figure 2.50 utilizes space more efficiently. The data span most of the range of the scales without getting too close to the scale lines. The data are the number of cigarettes consumed daily by a smoker in a 28-day program to quit smoking; after the 28 days the smoker quit altogether. A "day" is defined as starting at 6:00 a.m. and ending 24 hours later. The open circles are the days Monday to Friday and the closed circles are Saturdays and Sundays.

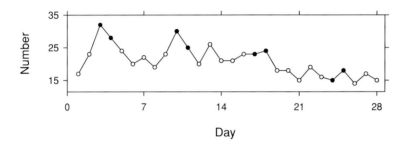

2.50 FILLING THE SCALE-LINE RECTANGLE. *Subject to the constraints that scales have, choose the scales so that the data rectangle fills up as much of the scale-line rectangle as possible.* This graph uses space efficiently. The line segments connecting successive plotting symbols are banked to 45°.

It is sometimes helpful to use the pair of scale lines for a variable to show two different scales.

The two scale lines for a variable on a graph provide an opportunity to show two different scales for the variable; the additional information of a second scale often can be helpful. One example is Figure 2.51. The data are the number of people in the United States in 1980 for each age from 0 to 84 [128]. The bottom horizontal scale line shows the age and the top horizontal scale line shows the year of birth.

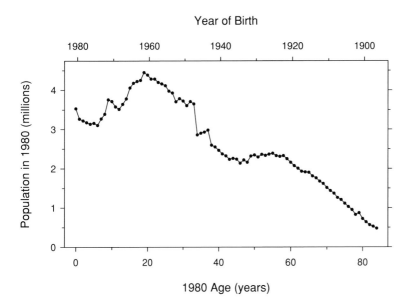

2.51 TWO SCALES. *It is sometimes helpful to use the pair of scale lines for a variable to show two different scales.* The bottom horizontal scale line shows age and the top horizontal scale line shows year of birth. The line segments connecting successive plotting symbols are banked to 45°.

When the logarithms of data are graphed there is an opportunity to use two scales. In Figure 2.52 the death rates for people 15 to 24 years old are graphed on a log scale. The bottom horizontal scale line shows log death rate in log deaths/million. The tick mark labels on this scale line allow us to see quickly by how much two values of the data differ in multiples of two. For example, the death rate due to automobile accidents is four times larger than that for suicide. The top scale line shows death rate on the original scale in deaths/million. This scale is added to allow an assessment of the magnitudes of the death rates without having to take powers of two in our heads.

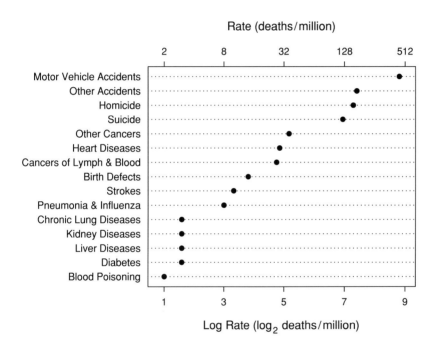

2.52 TWO SCALES. The bottom horizontal scale line shows log death rate in log deaths/million and the top horizontal scale line shows death rate in deaths/million.

When magnitudes are shown on a graph we can use two scales to show the data in their units of measurement and to show percent change from some baseline value. Figure 2.53 is a graph of averages of the mathematics Scholastic Aptitude Test scores for selected years from 1967 to 1982 [127]. The left vertical scale line shows the scores and the right vertical scale line shows percent change from 1967. Without the right scale it takes some mental arithmetic to determine the percent changes, for example, to see that the change from 1967 to 1982 was about 5%.

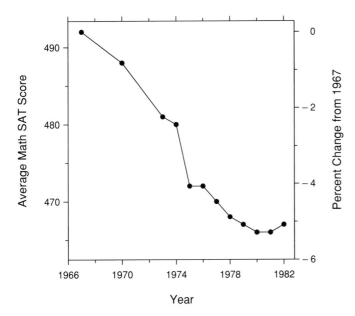

2.53 TWO SCALES. The left vertical scale line shows SAT score and the right vertical scale line shows percent change from 1967. The line segments connecting successive plotting symbols are banked to 45°.

Choose appropriate scales when data on different panels are compared.

Figure 2.54 shows data from an experiment on graphical perception [34]. A group of 51 subjects judged 40 pairs of values on bar charts and the same 40 pairs on pie charts; each judgment consisted of studying the two values and visually judging what percent the smaller was of the larger. The top panel of Figure 2.54 shows the 40 average judgment errors (averaged across subjects) graphed against the true percents for the 40 pie chart judgments. The bottom panel shows the same variables for the bar chart judgments. To enhance the comparison of the bar chart and pie chart values, the scales on the two panels are the same; this allows us to see very clearly that the pie chart judgments are less accurate than the bar chart judgments. One result of the common scale is that the data do not fill either panel; we should always be prepared to forego the fill principle to achieve an effective comparison. But note that if all of the data were put on one of the panels, the data rectangle would nearly fill the scale-line rectangle.

Using the same scales in the two panels of Figure 2.54 allows a number of quantitative comparisons to be made of the two sets of data. We can compare the average level of the absolute error of each chart type for each true percent. For example, we can see that the average level is about the same for true percents less than about 35%, but generally for percents greater than 35%, the average level is greater for pie charts. Furthermore, we can compare the variation in the errors for the two chart types. There is greater change in the pie chart errors than in the bar chart errors as the true percent changes; the pie chart errors increase but the bar chart errors have a flat pattern. The same scales can be used in this example, in part, because the overall levels of the two sets of data are not radically different.

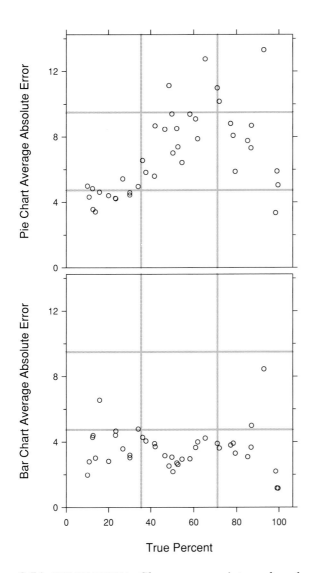

2.54 COMPARISON. *Choose appropriate scales when data on different panels are compared.* Scales on different panels should be made as commensurate as possible when the data on the different panels are compared. On this graph the scales on the top panel are the same as those on the bottom.

But suppose the overall levels of different data sets on a graph vary by a large amount. Figure 2.55 shows an example. The data are the winning times of four track races at the Olympics from 1900 to 1984 [17, 98]. The four lines have the same slopes but different intercepts and were fitted to the data using least-squares. The overall levels of the times are quite different; if the vertical scales were the same, the data on each panel would be contained in a very narrow horizontal band. Instead, the vertical scales vary, but the number of log seconds per cm is the same. This allows us to compare the rates of change of the four sets of log running times. For example, we can see that the overall rates of decrease through time for the four distances have been about the same. Since logs are graphed, this means that the percent reductions in the running times have been about the same. We can readily perceive the rate of change because the segments connecting the plotting symbols on the four panels are collectively banked to $45°$.

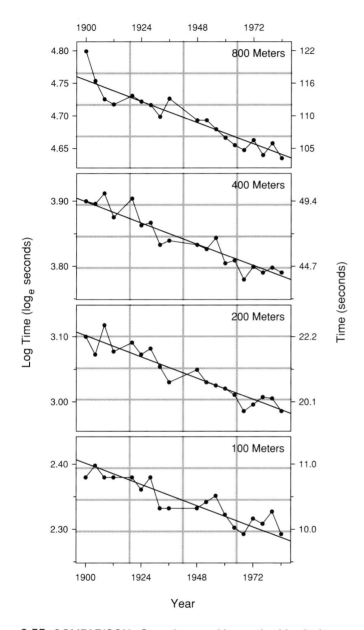

2.55 COMPARISON. Sometimes making scales identical prevents effects from being seen. The next best thing is illustrated on this graph — the number of units per cm is the same on the four vertical scales. The four lines on the panels have the same slope. The line segments connecting successive plotting symbols on the four panels are banked to 45°.

Sometimes even the number of units per cm cannot be the same without ruining our judgment of rate of change. In Figure 2.56, the data in the top left panel are the monthly measurements of atmospheric CO_2 concentrations that were discussed in Section 1.1 (pp. 6–9). The other panels graph frequency components of the data. The variation of the data in the bottom two panels is considerably less than that in the top two panels; were we to make the number of units per cm the same on all panels, the vertical scales of the bottom two panels would be too small. One way to appreciate the changes in the number of units per cm on the five panels is to study the tick mark labels and the distances between them, but this is a difficult visual operation. To make appreciation of the scale change easier, rectangles have been put to the right of the panels. The vertical lengths of the rectangles represent equal changes in parts per million on the five vertical scales.

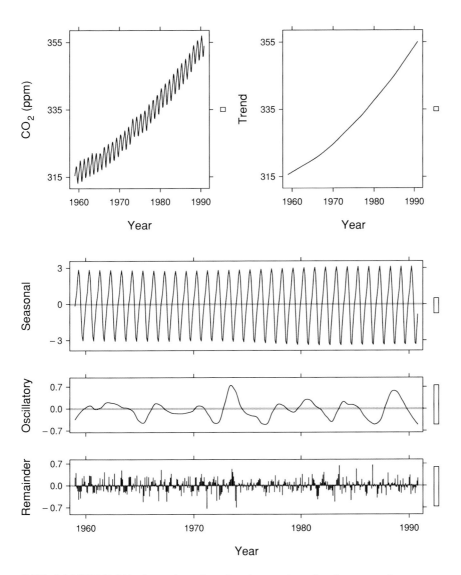

2.56 COMPARISON. Sometimes keeping the number of units per cm the same on different panels is not possible. On this graph the number of units per cm on the vertical scales varies. The rectangles on the right show the relative scaling; the vertical lengths represent the same change in ppm on the five vertical scales.

The left panel of Figure 2.59 graphs the CO_2 trend curve from
Figure 2.56. The sensible thing has been done; there is no zero and the
segments are banked to 45°. The right panel includes zero and the result
is ridiculous, even worse, misleading because the increase in the rate of
change of CO_2 with time is not readily perceived because the
orientations of the segments that make up the curve are so close to 0°.
Were we to attempt both banking to 45° and including 0, keeping the
width of the data rectangle the same, the height of the scale-line
rectangle would be 32 cm, clearly impractical.

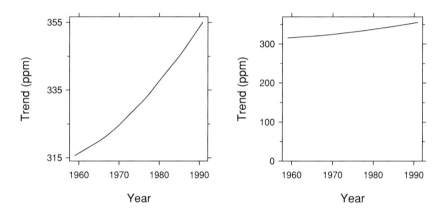

2.59 ZERO. *Do not insist that zero always be included on a scale showing
magnitude.* The left panel displays the trend curve sensibly; the curve is banked to 45°.
The right panel, which includes zero, does not allow effective judgment of the change
through time because the aspect ratio is too small.

When this zero issue is contemplated calmly, and examples such as
the previous ones are given, it all seems quite simple. For the CO_2 data,
one would expect the zero-line issue not to arise since the right panel of
Figure 2.59 is such a preposterous graph. But it did arise, and in a forum
of great importance. In March 1981 members of the U.S. Senate
convened scientists for testimony on global warming. There was an
exchange between U.S. Senator Albert Gore, Jr., trying to galvanize
scientists and politicians into action on global warming, and N. Douglas
Pewitt, a witness for the U.S. Department of Energy who was resisting
action. The exchange is described by Stephen Schneider in his book
Global Warming [108]. It needs no comment:

Gore responded that the Mauna Loa observatory data had clearly demonstrated increases in carbon dioxide and that it continued to show buildups. He pushed Pewitt further, "This is a rather impressive body of data that continues to accumulate. Doesn't that lead you to look at it in a different light?"

. . . Pewitt came back to the Mauna Loa CO_2 trend chart, calling it very deceptive: "It is a clever piece of chartology, in that it is intellectually accurate but can be subject to being read the wrong way." Gore was incredulous, and countered, pointing out that "if you look at a longer-range chart going back to 1880, you see virtually the same thing . . ." Gore continued, "Dr. Pewitt, I don't want to put words in your mouth, but I got the impression that you were saying the significance of the chart should be substantially discounted."

Pewitt responded, "No. What I said is that that is chartology. It is intellectually just exactly correct. It displays 315 going to 336, but it appears to be going from 0 to very large amounts."

Gore was stunned. "It is clearly labeled 316 to . . ."

Pewitt interrupted, "That is correct, and a person very careful in their review of this chart will see that it is true. That is the reason why I said it was intellectually correct. I mean, it is objectively a statement of fact that is true. The impression it leaves on some people is quite a different impression. I have always had trouble playing with chartology. It appears to be going from nothing to a vast amount and that is a fact. We have a lawyer here who is nodding in agreement — it is true."

By this time most of us in the hearing room were giggling at this double talk. Gore simply read into the record the entire CO_2 emission chart from 1860 through 1980 and gave up the debate on that point.

Use a logarithmic scale when it is important to understand percent change or multiplicative factors.

There are some who feel that including a zero line on a graph helps us to better understand percent change and multiplicative factors. Darrell Huff [61] states that a graph with a zero baseline is beneficial "because the whole graph is in proportion and there is a zero line at the bottom for comparison. Your ten percent *looks* like ten percent."

It may well be that a zero line contributes a little to such judgments, but our ability to judge percents and factors is at best extremely poor. If we want to make such judgments it is far better to take logarithms. Suppose a, b, c, and d are all positive numbers with $a/b = c/d$ and b a few times bigger than d. Then on a graph of the four numbers it is quite hard to judge that the ratios are equal because on the graph, b is further from a than c is from d. This is illustrated in Figure 2.60. The data are the number of telephones in the U.S. from 1935 to 1970 [126]. The zero line is there, but it is very difficult to judge percents. Consider the following basic question: how is the percent increase in phones changing through time? For example, how does the percent change from 1935 to 1953, the middle of the time period, compare with the percent change from 1953 to 1970? It is very difficult to judge from Figure 2.60 without reading off values from the vertical scale and doing arithmetic.

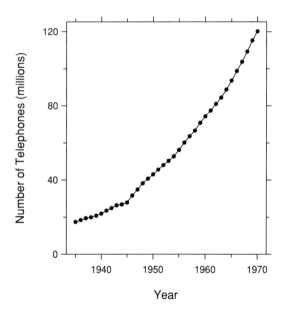

2.60 LOGS FOR FACTORS. The data are the number of telephones in the United States each year from 1935 to 1970. It is nearly impossible to judge whether the percentage increase is constant, decreasing, or increasing. The line segments connecting successive plotting symbols are banked to 45°.

When magnitudes are graphed on a logarithmic scale, percents and factors are easier to judge since equal multiplicative factors and percents result in equal distances throughout the entire scale. For our four numbers above,

$$\log(b) - \log(a) = \log(c) - \log(d) .$$

So $\log(b)$ is the same distance along the log scale from $\log(a)$ as $\log(c)$ is from $\log(d)$. This is illustrated in Figure 2.61. A log base 2 scale is used on the vertical scale for the telephone data. Now we can see that the percent increase in telephones through time has been roughly stable, since the trend in the data is roughly linear. Now we can see easily that telephones increased from 1935 to 1953 by about the same factor $(2^{1.5} \approx 2.8)$ as they did from 1953 to 1970.

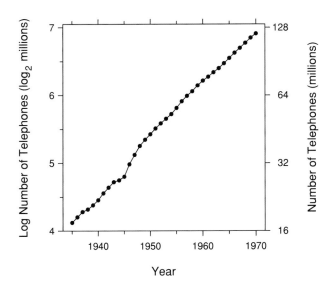

2.61 LOGS FOR FACTORS. *Use a logarithmic scale when it is important to understand percent change or multiplicative factors.* The data in Figure 2.60, are graphed by taking logarithms base 2. Now it is clear that the percentage increase in telephones was roughly stable from 1935 to 1970. The line segments connecting successive plotting symbols are banked to 45°.

Many phenomena obey multiplicative laws, even laws of aircraft engagement in battle, as Winston Churchill discovered. Churchill, known to all as a person of prodigious talent in matters of state, was remarkably facile in quantitative thinking. As an historian, he liberally used tables, graphs, and maps. For example in his epic account, *The Second World War*, there are 96 diagrams of military operations, 62 tables, 17 graphs, and 37 maps [19].

Churchill's discussion of the Battle of Britain in *Their Finest Hour*, the third volume of *The Second World War*, reveals the multiplicative law. This battle, fought between the Luftwaffe and the R.A.F. from July to October of 1940, until then a dark period for the British who suffered loss after loss, established British air superiority over the South of England and the English Channel. This was a turning point, a first demonstration that the German war machine was not invincible. A British loss in this air battle would have meant an imminent German invasion of the British Isles and a near-certain loss of the war. Churchill writes:

> Our fate now depended upon victory in the air. The German leaders had recognized that all their plans for the invasion of Britain depended on winning air supremacy above the Channel and the chosen landing places on our south coast.

Later in his account, Churchill analyzes the German and British losses, referring to a table of data that is reproduced in Figure 2.62:

> In cold blood, with the knowledge of the after-time, we may study the actual losses of the British and German Air Forces in what may well be deemed one of the decisive battles of the world. From the table on page 339 our hopes and fears may be contrasted with what happened.
>
> No doubt we were always oversanguine in our estimates of enemy scalps. In the upshot we got two to one of the German assailants, instead of three to one, as we believed and declared.

In the last sentence, Churchill characterizes the losses as "two to one" German losses to British losses and "three to one" estimated German losses to British losses. Presumably these numbers came from the totals at the bottom of his table:

$$\frac{1733 \text{ actual German losses}}{915 \text{ actual British losses}} = 1.89 \approx 2$$

$$\frac{2698 \text{ estimated German losses}}{915 \text{ actual British losses}} = 2.95 \approx 3 \ .$$

Thus Churchill chose to quote factors of 2 and 3 rather than absolute differences of losses. Because

$$1733 - 915 = 818 \approx 800$$

and

$$2698 - 915 = 1783 \approx 1800$$

he might have written, "In the upshot we got 800 more than they, instead of 1800, as we believed and declared." But Churchill saw multiplicative factors as the right way to think.

Aircraft Losses

	British Fighters Lost by R.A.F. (complete write-off or missing)	Enemy Aircraft Actually DESTROYED (according to German records)	Enemy Aircraft CLAIMED by us (Fighter Command, A.A., Balloons, etc.)
WEEKLY TOTALS:			
July 10–13	15	45	63
Week to July 20	22	31	49
Week to July 27	14	51	58
Week to Aug. 3	8	56	39
Week to Aug. 10	25	44	64
Week to Aug. 17	134	261	496
Week to Aug. 24	59	145	251
Week to Aug. 31	141	193	316
Week to Sep. 7	144	187	375
Week to Sep. 14	67	102	182
Week to Sep. 21	52	120	268
Week to Sep. 28	72	118	230
Week to Oct. 5	44	112	100
Week to Oct. 12	47	73	66
Week to Oct. 19	29	67	38
Week to Oct. 26	21	72	43
Oct. 27–31	21	56	60
MONTHLY TOTALS:			
July (from July 10)	58	164	203
August	*360*	*662*	*1133*
September	*361*	*582*	*1108*
October	136	325	254
Totals	*915*	*1733*	*2698*

2.62 LOGS FOR FACTORS. Churchill's table shows British and German aircraft losses in World War II.

It makes sense for us to think in terms of factors, as Churchill did, and take logs in looking further at these data. This is done in Figure 2.65 where weekly losses are graphed against time to see the course of the Battle of Britain as it unfolded during those crucial months.

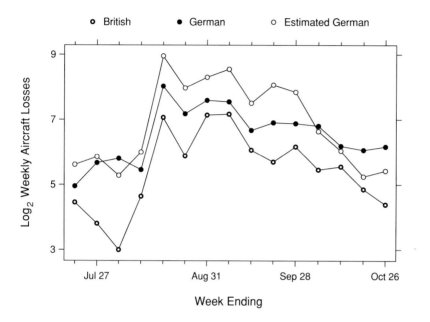

2.65 LOGS FOR FACTORS. The logs of aircraft losses are graphed against time. The line segments connecting successive plotting symbols are banked to 45°.

Churchill's quantitative analysis — dispassionate, objective, and on target — then concludes with the eloquence that we expect of him:

> At the summit the stamina and valour of our fighter pilots remained unconquerable and supreme. Thus Britain was saved. Well might I say in the House of Commons, "Never in the field of human conflict was so much owed by so many to so few."

Showing data on a logarithmic scale can cure skewness toward large values.

It is common for positive data to be *skewed toward large values*: some values bunch together at the low end of the scale and others trail off to the high end with increasing gaps between the values as they get higher. Severe skewness causes most of the data to be squashed into a narrow interval, which degrades our judgment of the data. An example of skewed data is given in Figure 2.66. The graph shows the 14 most abundant elements in stone meteorites [47]; the data are the average percent of each of the elements. Our judgment of the relative values of the data is poor because the ten smallest percents vary over a small range.

A common remedy for skewness is to take logarithms. Indeed, it is the frequent success of this remedy that partly accounts for the large use of logarithms in graphical data display. Figure 2.67 shows the meteorite data on a log scale; now the distribution is much more nearly uniform and we can more effectively judge the data.

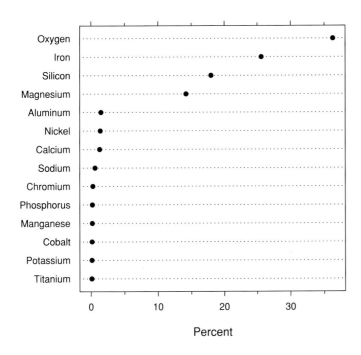

2.66 LOGS FOR SKEWNESS. Because the data on this graph are severely skewed, we cannot accurately judge the relative values of the data.

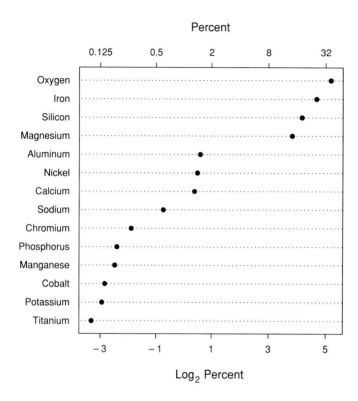

Percent

2.67 LOGS FOR SKEWNESS. *Showing data on a logarithmic scale can cure skewness toward large values.* The logs of the data in Figure 2.66 are graphed, which has eliminated the skewness.

Use a scale break only when necessary. If a break cannot be avoided, use a full scale break. Do not connect numerical values on two sides of a break. Taking logs can cure the need for a break.

Figure 2.68 shows the iridium data discussed in Section 2.3 (pp. 54–66). Two *full scale breaks* are used to signal changes on the horizontal scale; the middle panel has a smaller number of data units per cm. The widths of the rectangles at the top of the graph portray the same number of data units on the panels.

A change or gap in a scale is shown forcefully by a full break. Some indicate a change or gap in the scale of a graph by a *partial scale break*: two short wavy parallel curves or two short parallel line segments breaking a scale line. This is illustrated on the horizontal scale line of the left panel in Figure 2.69 [101]. But the partial scale break is a weak indicator that the reader can fail to appreciate fully; visually, the graph is still a single panel that invites the viewer to see patterns between the two scales.

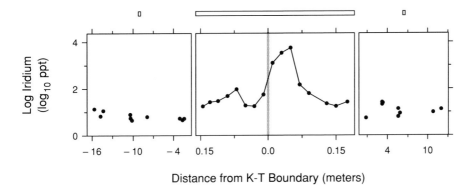

Distance from K-T Boundary (meters)

2.68 SCALE BREAKS. *Use a scale break only when necessary. If a break cannot be avoided, use a full scale break. Do not connect numerical values on two sides of a break. Taking logs can cure the need for a break.* This graph uses full scale breaks on the horizontal scale to signal changes in the number of units per cm. The full breaks show the scale breaks forcefully. Without the breaks, the data in the center panel would lie very nearly on a vertical line and there would be no time resolution. The rectangles at the top of the graph portray the same number of horizontal scale units on each panel.

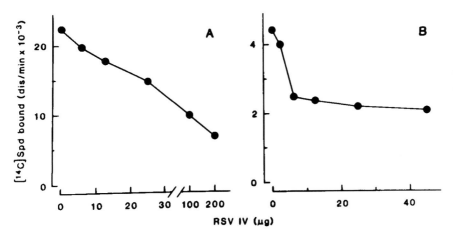

2.69 SCALE BREAKS. The partial scale break on the horizontal scale of the left panel does not give a forceful indication of a break. The connection of numerical values across the break gives the misleading impression that the data are roughly linear.

Numerical values should not be connected across a break. In the left panel of Figure 2.69, the connection across the break gives the misleading impression that the data are roughly linear across the entire horizontal scale; in fact the slope of the values decreases as the variable on the horizontal scale increases, as shown by Figure 2.70, which graphs the data with no scale break.

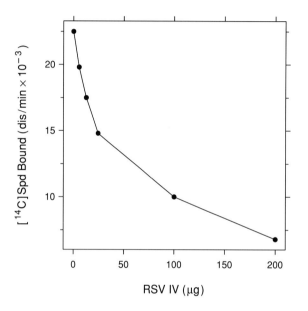

2.70 SCALE BREAKS. The data from the left panel of Figure 2.69 are graphed without a scale break. Now it is clear that the data are not roughly linear and that the slope decreases as the variable on the horizontal scale increases. The line segments connecting successive plotting symbols are banked to 45°.

Figures 2.71 and 2.72 show other bad breaks. Figure 2.71 [87] gives a misleading impression because the continuation of the lines across the break has no meaning. The tick marks on the horizontal scale are labeled 3, 10, and 30; since the logarithms of these values are nearly equally spaced, the authors presumably intended a horizontal log scale. The three lines give the impression that the pattern of each data set is linear through the origin. But a value of zero U/ml of interferon is off at minus infinity on the horizontal log scale, so the three lines could not possibly go through the origin. In Figure 2.72 [111] bars and error bars are allowed to barge right through two scale breaks. The bar lengths and areas, important and prominent visual aspects of the graph, are meaningless.

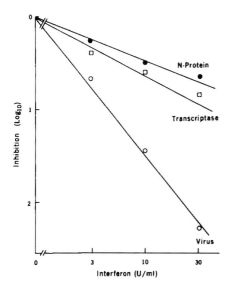

2.71 SCALE BREAKS. On this graph the lines drawn through the partial scale break have no meaning and give the misleading impression that the pattern of the data goes linearly through the origin. Since the horizontal scale is logarithmic, zero is actually at minus infinity.

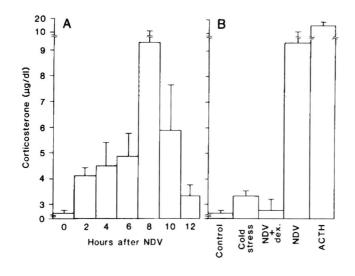

2.72 SCALE BREAKS. The lengths of the bars that barge right through the scale breaks have no meaning.

Full scale breaks should be used only when necessary. Figure 2.70 shows the break of Figure 2.69 is not needed. Taking logarithms of the data can often relieve the need for a scale break. Figure 2.73 shows data from William Playfair's *Statistical Breviary* [105], published in 1801. The data, which are the populations of 22 European cities, are forced into a small region of the scale. Figure 2.74 graphs the data with a break. True, the data are now not squashed, but we have paid a great price. The values in the right panel cannot be graphically compared with those on the left. The best we can do is a tedious table look-up by reading the scales of each panel. Figure 2.75 uses a log scale, a better solution than the broken scale because all of the data can be readily visually compared.

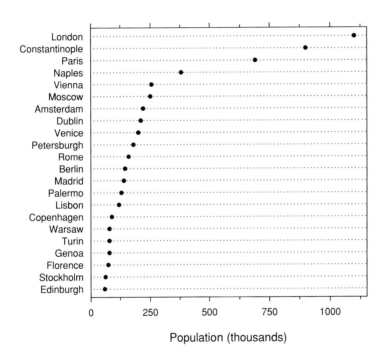

2.73 LOGS. The dot plot graphs populations of 22 European cities. The data are skewed to the right, which degrades the resolution of the graphed values.

Population (thousands)

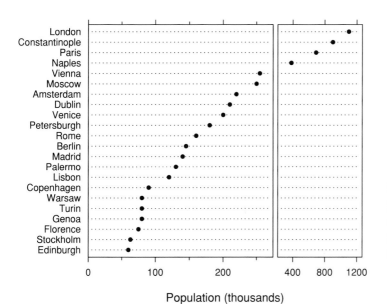

2.74 LOGS. The populations are graphed with a scale break. This prevents graphical comparison of all values.

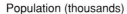

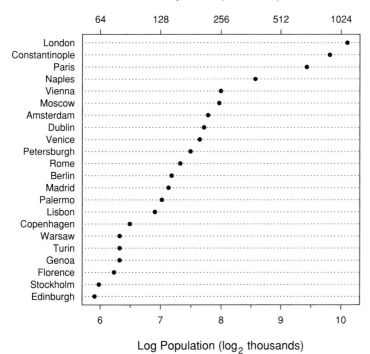

2.75 LOGS. The populations are graphed on a log scale, which relieves the need for a scale break.

2.6   General Strategy

Graphing is much like writing. Our written language has grammatical and syntactical rules that govern the details of word and sentence construction; most of the graphical principles in the previous sections — Clear Vision, Clear Understanding, Banking to 45°, and Scales — are analogous to these rules. But there are also more general guidelines — that is, overall strategies — for writing; these are more nebulous rules aimed at producing clear, interesting prose. For example, William Strunk Jr. and E. B. White [115] encourage clarity by "Use definite, specific, concrete language," and encourage brevity by "Do not overwrite." The first two principles of this chapter — make the data stand out and avoid superfluity — are general strategies for graphs. (Note the similarity between the two Strunk and White principles and these two general graphical principles. Edward R. Tufte once made the insightful remark that Strunk and White's book on the elements of writing is one of the best treatises on graphing data.) In this section several general strategies for graphing data are discussed.

A large amount of quantitative information can be packed into a small region.

Previous principles in this chapter have stipulated that graphs should not be cluttered and should not have superfluous elements, but this does *not* preclude a large amount of quantitative information being shown on a graph, even a small graph. It is possible to put a large data set on a graph in an uncluttered way. Figure 2.76, the graph of the CO_2 data and its four components that we have seen before, is an example. There are 396 monthly data points on each of the panels of this graph, which is 1920 points altogether. Each data point consists of two numbers, a value on the horizontal scale and a value on the vertical scale. Thus 3840 numbers are shown on this graph.

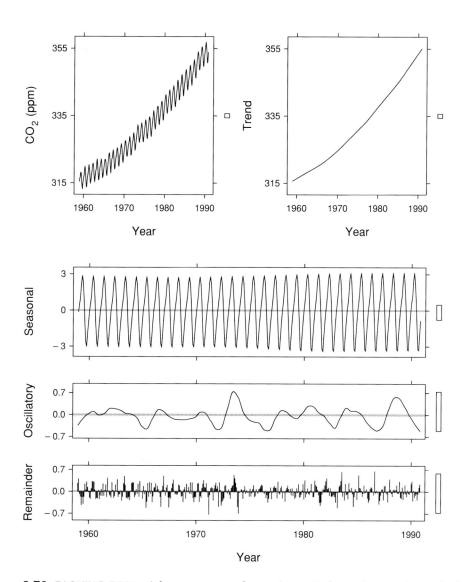

2.76 PACKING DATA. *A large amount of quantitative information can be packed into a small region.* The computer graphics revolution has given us the capability to graph a large amount of quantitative information in a small space. There are 1920 data points on this graph; each portrays two numerical values, so 3840 numbers are shown.

Graph data two or more times when it is needed.

A corollary of the previous principle on iteration is that, whether we are in the mode of analyzing data or presenting data to others, we should not hesitate to make two or more graphs of the same data. Two different ways of graphing data sometimes bring out aspects that only one way cannot. For example, in a presentation of the doctorate degree data of Figure 2.77, it would be entirely sensible to use Graph 2 and Graph 4; both show interesting aspects of the data. Figure 2.78, shown earlier in Sections 2.2 (pp. 30–55) and 2.4 (pp. 63-73), is another example. Each of the three sets of data is shown twice. Graphing each data set separately in the left three panels allows the error bars to be perceived without interfering with one another. Graphing the three data sets together in the right panel allows them to be more effectively compared.

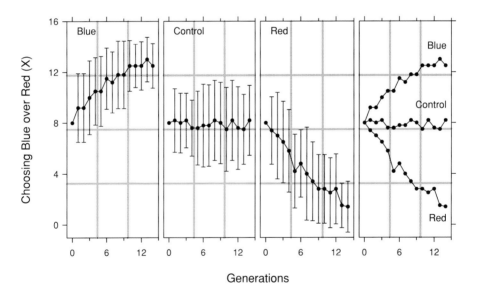

2.78 REGRAPHING. *Graph data two or more times when it is needed.* Each data set is graphed twice, once in one of the three left panels to allow an unobstructed view of the error bars and once in the right panel to allow an effective comparison of the data sets.

Many useful graphs require careful, detailed study.

There are some who argue that a graph is a success only if the important information in the data can be seen within a few seconds. While there is a place for rapidly-understood graphs, it is too limiting to make speed a requirement in science and technology, where the use of graphs ranges from detailed, in-depth data analysis to quick presentation. The next two graphs illustrate these extremes.

Cyril Burt was a giant in psychology until his world began to crumble in 1974, three years after his death. Burt was one of the leading proponents of the theory that intelligence, as measured by IQ scores, is largely inherited. Burt's data strongly supported this view — too strongly, as it turns out. In 1974 suspicions were raised about the authenticity of some of Burt's data and his analyses [70]. For five years doubts about Burt's integrity grew, culminating in a biography by Hearnshaw who concluded, as others already had, that Burt faked much of his data, invented collaborators, and sent letters to journals from fictitious people who supported his work [58].

Table 2.1 shows data that Burt published in 1961 in the *British Journal of Statistical Psychology* [15]. The numbers are part of a larger data set that were widely quoted in subsequent scientific work until D. D. Dorfman, a psychologist at the University of Iowa, gave a convincing argument in 1978 that the numbers were made-up, either in whole or in part [46]. The values in Table 2.1 were purported to be mean IQ scores of 40,000 father-child pairs divided into six social classes.

Table 2.1 CYRIL BURT DATA.

	Adult Mean IQ	Child Mean IQ
Higher Professional	139.7	120.8
Lower Professional	130.6	114.7
Clerical	115.9	107.8
Skilled	108.2	104.6
Semiskilled	97.8	98.9
Unskilled	84.9	92.6

The data in Table 2.1 look innocent enough until they are graphed. Figure 2.79 is a graph of the mean scores for the children against the corresponding values for adults. The impugnment of these data is based, in part, on the notion that the mean scores are simply too good to be true. In 1959, J. Conway [39] had put forward the equation

$$\text{child score } - 100 = 0.5 \, (\text{adult score } - 100)$$

as a method for predicting the mean IQ score of children in a given class from the mean IQ score of the fathers in the class; this predictive line is shown in Figure 2.79. The line lies extraordinarily close to the data. Thus for Burt's data, Conway's predictive method, with its mathematically elegant coefficient of 0.5, makes nearly perfect predictions.

Figure 2.79 requires only a quick look to absorb the important quantitative information. The main message — that the mean scores are very close to the line — can be absorbed almost instantaneously.

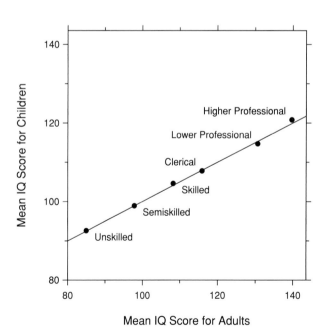

2.79 DETAILED STUDY. The important information on this graph, that Cyril Burt's fictitious data lie very close to the line, can be extracted with just a quick look.

Some graphs, however, require long and detailed scrutinizing. This is entirely reasonable. The important criterion for a graph is not simply how fast we can see a result; rather, it is whether through the use of the graph we can see something that would have been harder to see otherwise or that could not have been seen at all. If a graphical display requires hours of study to make a discovery that would have gone undetected without the graph, then the display is a success.

Figure 2.80 is a graph that requires detailed study. The graphical method used in the figure, an exceedingly useful one called a *scatterplot matrix*, will be discussed in Section 3.9 (pp. 193–197). The data in Figure 2.80 are measurements of four variables: wind speed, temperature, solar radiation at ground level, and concentrations of the air pollutant, ozone [13]. There is one measurement of each variable on each of 111 days.

Each panel of Figure 2.80 is a scatterplot of one variable against another. For the three panels in the bottom row, the vertical scale is ozone, and the three horizontal scales are solar radiation, temperature, and wind speed. So the graph in position (2,1) in the matrix — that is, the second column and first row — is a scatterplot of ozone against solar radiation; position (3,1) is a scatterplot of ozone against temperature; position (4,1) is a scatterplot of ozone against wind speed.

The scatterplot matrix reveals much about the four variables. A discussion of what is seen, since it is long and detailed, will be postponed to the full discussion of scatterplot matrices in Section 3.9 (pp. 193–197); it suffices to say here that the revelations come only after careful, detailed study of the graph. It might well be expected that a graph with 1332 points on it, each encoding two numbers for a total of 2662 numbers, would require careful study.

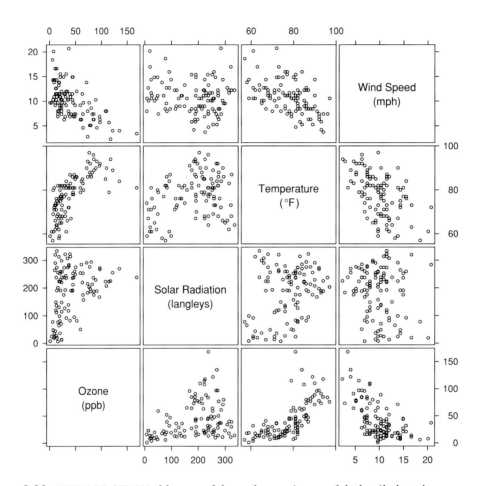

2.80 DETAILED STUDY. *Many useful graphs require careful, detailed study.*
Compared with that needed for Figure 2.79, this scatterplot matrix of ozone and
meteorological measurements requires lengthy study to extract the information. But the
lengthy study reveals information that would be very difficult or impossible to get by other
means.

3 Graphical Methods

This chapter is about graphical methods: types of graphs and ways of encoding quantitative information on graphs. The methods allow us to analyze both the overall structure of the data and the detail of the data.

Section 3.1 (pp. 120–126) discusses the logarithm, a basic tool that is useful in all areas of graphical data analysis.

Section 3.2 (pp. 126–132) is about another basic tool of data display — graphing residuals from the fit of a mathematical function to a set of data.

Section 3.3 (pp. 132–149) is about distributions. Suppose we have one or more sets of measurements of a single quantitative variable. The graphical methods of the section display the distribution of the data — where the measurements lie along the measurement scale.

Section 3.4 (pp. 150–154) is about dot plots, which display measurements of a quantitative variable where each measurement has a label. When the labels are a cross-classification of two or more categorical variables, the display becomes a multiway dot plot.

Section 3.5 (pp. 154–165) is about plotting symbols and curve types on graphs with two quantitative variables, a mundane issue for data display but an issue filled with problems that need methods. In Section 2.2 (pp. 25–54) we saw that two-variable graphs can easily fail because graphical elements are obscured or different data sets are not easily visually assembled. The methods of the section attack these problems.

Section 3.6 (pp. 166–167) shows how visual reference grids enhance our comparison of data on the different panels of a graph with two or more juxtaposed panels.

Section 3.7 (pp. 168–180) is about loess, a method for fitting curves to scatterplots. When the purpose of a scatterplot is made to study how one variable, a response, depends on another variable, a factor, noise in the data often makes it difficult to visually assess the underlying pattern. A smooth curve can show the pattern much more clearly.

Section 3.8 (pp. 180–192) discusses graphical methods for time series, which occur commonly in all areas of science and technology.

Section 3.9 (pp. 193–197) introduces the scatterplot matrix, an important method for the display of measurements of three or more quantitative variables.

Section 3.10 (pp. 198–202) is about the coplot, another method for displaying three or more quantitative variables. In this section, the tool is used to display scattered measurements of three variables.

Section 3.11 (pp. 203–205) continues with the coplot. In this section it is used to display a function of two variables, which is a surface in three dimensions.

Section 3.12 (pp. 206–209) is about brushing, a direct manipulation method in which graphical elements on a computer screen are changed in real time by an input device such as a mouse.

Section 3.13 (pp. 209–212) is about color. There are two uses of color for data display that genuinely enhance the visual decoding of information — encoding different collections of graphical elements by different colors, and encoding a quantitative variable on a color level plot.

Section 3.14 (pp. 212–220) is about statistical variation. There is a general discussion of the empirical variation in data and the sample-to-sample variation of a statistic computed from data. Two-tiered error bars are introduced for showing sample-to-sample variation.

3.1   Logarithms

Logarithms are one of man's most useful inventions. They are indispensable in science and technology and are a vital part of graphical methods. Their usefulness has been amply illustrated earlier in the book — for improving resolution and for showing data where percents and factors are important.

In Figure 3.1, logarithms of the maximum amounts of solar radiation penetrating ocean water at various ocean depths are graphed against depth [84]. The least-squares fit to the data is also shown. At one time it was presumed that plant life did not exist in the ocean below about 200 meters because of low light intensity. But scientists at the Smithsonian Institution in Washington, D.C. and the Harbor Branch Foundation in Florida discovered an alga at a depth of 268 meters in waters off the coast of San Salvador Island in the Bahamas. The filled circles in Figure 3.1 are measurements of radiation that the discoverers presented in their paper, and the open circles are values that they extrapolated from the measured values. The line on the graph is the least-squares line fitted to the measured values.

Logarithms are useful here because radiation changes by five powers of ten from about 10^3 at sea level to about 10^{-2} at 268 meters. Also, it is natural to use a log scale because we would expect attenuation of the solar radiation, if the transmission properties of the ocean water are relatively constant, to be multiplicative as a function of depth; if s is the radiation at sea level and f is the fraction of radiation remaining after passing through one centimeter of ocean water, then the radiation at a depth of one centimeter is $r(1) = fs$, at two centimeters is $r(2) = f^2s$,

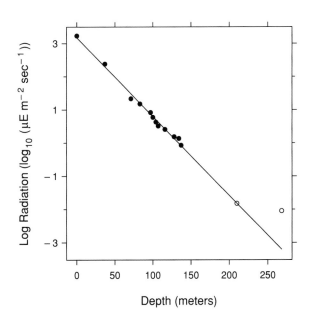

3.1 LOG BASE 10. Graphing data on a log base 10 scale is reasonable when the data go through many powers of 10, as on the vertical scale of this graph.

and at d centimeters is $r(d) = f^d s$. On a log scale, radiation is

$$\log(r(d)) = d\log(f) + \log(s)$$

and is thus a linear function of d. Figure 3.1 shows such an attenuation process is commensurate with the log measurements, which are roughly linear with depth. The extrapolated radiation value at 210 meters fits the pattern of the measured values, but the extrapolated value at 268 meters does not; either the ocean water changes its properties or there has been a faulty extrapolation.

Log Base 2 and Log Base e

Log base 10 is almost always used in scientific graphs for a log scale. This is much too limiting. Log base 2 and log base e (natural logarithms) should always be considered. Using a different base does not change the pattern of the points but changes only the values at the tick marks because the logarithm of one base is just a constant times the logarithm of another base. The relationship between log base b and log base c is

$$\log_c(x) = \log_b(x)/\log_b(c) \, .$$

Thus

$$\log_2(x) = \log_{10}(x)/\log_{10}(2)$$

and

$$\log_e(x) = \log_{10}(x)/\log_{10}(e) \, .$$

The choice of the base depends on the range of the data values that need to be visually compared. Suppose the data go through many powers of 10, as the radiation data in Figure 3.1 do. In such a case it is reasonable to use log base 10. But suppose the data range over two powers of 10 or less. This is the case in Figure 3.2; the data are the number of telephones in the United States [126]. In such a case it is inevitable that equally spaced tick marks for log base 10 will involve fractional powers of 10, as Figure 3.2 illustrates. It is difficult to deal with such fractional powers. It is easy enough to remember $10^{0.5}$ is a little bigger than 3, but to keep many fractional powers of 10 in our heads and try to use them to study a graph is cumbersome. In such a situation it makes sense to convert to log base 2 as in Figure 3.3. It is easier to deal with powers of 2 than fractional powers of 10. For example, we can see that the number of phones increased by a factor of about 4 from 1935 to 1960.

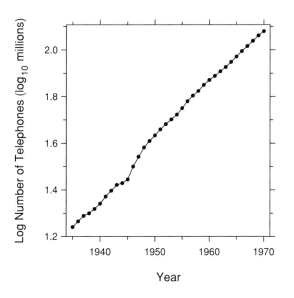

3.2 LOG BASE 10. The data, a time series of the number of telephones in the United States, are graphed on a log base 10 scale. When the data range through two or fewer powers of 10, the log base 10 scale is not as informative since we must deal with fractional powers of 10, as on this graph. The line segments connecting successive plotting symbols are banked to 45°.

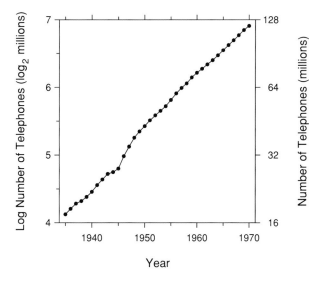

3.3 LOG BASE 2. When the data go through a small number of powers of 10, log base 2 often provides a useful scale. The left vertical scale line shows the data in log units and the right vertical scale line shows the original units. The line segments connecting successive plotting symbols are banked to 45°.

Now

$$d = \log_e(v) - \log_e(u) = \log_e\left(\frac{v}{u}\right) = \log_e(1 + r) \, .$$

But if d is small,

$$\log_e(1 + r) \approx r$$

and therefore

$$d \approx r \, .$$

Here are several values of r and d:

$$\log_e(1 + 0.05) = 0.049 \qquad \log_e(1 - 0.05) = -0.051$$
$$\log_e(1 + 0.1) \; = 0.095 \qquad \log_e(1 - 0.1) \; = -0.105$$
$$\log_e(1 + 0.15) = 0.140 \qquad \log_e(1 - 0.15) = -0.163$$
$$\log_e(1 + 0.2) \; = 0.182 \qquad \log_e(1 - 0.2) \; = -0.223$$
$$\log_e(1 + 0.25) = 0.223 \qquad \log_e(1 - 0.25) = -0.288$$

When d is greater than 0.25 or less than -0.25, the approximation is less accurate and is not as useful.

It is, of course, considerably harder to go back mentally to the original scale from a natural log scale than from base 2 or 10. We know readily what 2^3 and 10^3 are, but e^3 is harder. For this reason it is often helpful to use one scale line to show the original scale, as illustrated in Figure 3.4.

3.2   Residuals

William Playfair, who was part statistical scientist and part political thinker, was the first person to study graphical data display and to experiment with graphical methods in a broad and serious way. He invented many types of graphs that are in use today. His *Commercial and Political Atlas* of 1786 [104] and his subsequent publications contain time series graphs, bar charts, pie charts, and graphs with data encoded by circle areas and line lengths. However, some of Playfair's inventions did not work, as will be demonstrated in Chapter 4.

In Playfair's *Statistical Breviary* [105], the populations of 22 cities are displayed by an area encoding; 22 circles are drawn whose areas are approximately proportional to the populations. The display is beautifully reproduced by Tufte [121]. The graph also contains a table of the populations, so we can compare the data and the areas of the circles.

Let Y_i be the circle areas and let X_i be the populations. If the areas encoded the data exactly we would have

$$Y_i = KX_i \ \text{ for } i = 1 \text{ to } 22 \ ,$$

which on a log base 2 scale is

$$\log_2(Y_i) = \log_2(X_i) + \log_2(K)$$

or

$$y_i = x_i + k \ .$$

In the top panel of Figure 3.5, y_i is graphed against x_i. Areas are relative to the area of the smallest circle, that for Edinburgh, in Playfair's display; that is, one unit of area is equal to the area of the Edinburgh circle. If the encoding by circle area were exact the points on the graph would lie on a line with slope one. But the points deviate from a line. The line drawn in the top panel is a least-squares fit with the slope constrained to be one. The vertical deviations of the points from the line, which are called *residuals*, tell us by how much the actual areas deviate from a perfect encoding. But it is difficult to assess the residuals because the points of the graph lie in a narrow band around the line.

Our judgment of the residuals can be greatly enhanced by graphing them against x_i. This is done in the bottom panel of Figure 3.5. The residuals are now more spread out since we have removed the overall linear effect. The scale of the residuals has been switched from log base 2 to log base e; we can interpret the residuals as percent deviations because all residuals are between -0.25 and 0.25 $\log_e$ units. The largest residual is about 0.15, which means the area of the circle corresponding to the value is about 15% larger than the ideal area of the fitted line. The smallest residual is about -0.15. Thus the percent deviations of the actual areas from the ideal ones range between about -15% and 15%.

There is another situation where graphing residuals is helpful. Suppose y_i is graphed against x_i, for $i = 1$ to n. Suppose y_i and x_i have the same units of measurement and our goal is to determine how much larger or smaller the y_i values are than the x_i values. An example is shown in the top panel of Figure 3.7. The data on the vertical scale, y_i, are the logarithms of abundances of certain elements in rocks brought back from the moon's Mare Tranquillitatis by the Apollo 11 astronauts in 1969 [86]. The data on the horizontal scale, x_i, are the logarithms of abundances of the same elements in basalt from the earth. The purpose of the graph is to see how the composition of the moon rocks compares with that of basalt.

In studying the composition data we would like to understand the values of $y_i - x_i$, the amounts by which the abundances differ. On the top panel of Figure 3.7, $y_i - x_i$ is equal to the vertical deviation of the point $(x_i,\ y_i)$ from the line $y = x$, and $x_i - y_i$ is equal to the horizontal deviation of $(x_i,\ y_i)$ from the line. As with other graphs, however, it is difficult to assess the values of these deviations, or residuals.

In Figure 3.5, where we studied Playfair's data, our purpose was to see how the areas, y_i, *depend on* the population measurements, x_i. For the abundance data in the top panel of Figure 3.7 the situation is different. Neither variable is dependent or independent; we are seeking simply to see how the two variables are related, and by how much the abundances differ. We might look at residuals, in analogy with the Playfair data, by graphing $y_i - x_i$ against x_i. This, however, does not treat x_i and y_i equally, and we could just as well graph $y_i - x_i$ against y_i.

One way to graph $y_i - x_i$ that takes the equivalence of x_i and y_i into account is the *Tukey mean-difference plot*: $y_i - x_i$ is graphed against $(y_i + x_i)/2$, as illustrated in the bottom panel of Figure 3.7. The mean-difference plot can be thought of as the result of rotating the points in the top panel by $45°$ in a clockwise direction and then allowing the rotated points to expand in the vertical direction to fill the data region. To see this suppose

$$u_i = (y_i + x_i)/\sqrt{2}$$

and

$$v_i = (y_i - x_i)/\sqrt{2}\,.$$

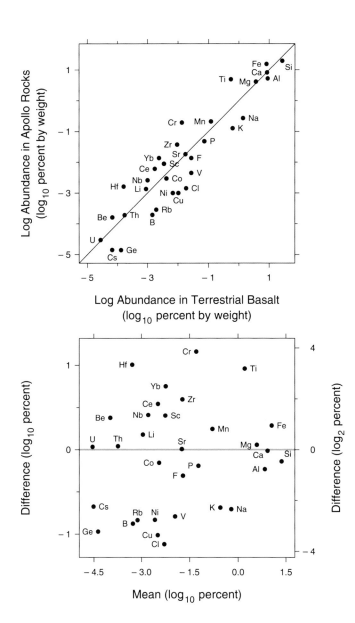

3.7 TUKEY MEAN-DIFFERENCE PLOT. In the top panel two sets of data with the same measurement scale are graphed to see how close the corresponding values are. The bottom panel is the Tukey mean-difference plot.

If we graphed v_i against u_i and kept the number of data units per cm the same as on the graph of y_i vs. x_i, the points on the new graph would be exactly a 45° clockwise rotation of the points on the old one. The reader can rotate the book page 45° clockwise to see how the configuration of points on this new graph would appear. In the Tukey mean-difference plot, the factor $1/\sqrt{2}$ for u_i is replaced by $1/2$, and the factor $1/\sqrt{2}$ for v_i is replaced by 1. Also, the number of data units per cm for $y_i - x_i$ is not

Another standard method for studying distributions is the *histogram,* one of the staples of scientific graphics that has a long history going back at least to the 19th century. In Figure 3.9 the stereogram times are shown by histograms. The variable on the vertical scales is percent of counts — 100 times the number of counts in each interval divided by the total number of observations, which is 43 for the NV times and 35 for the VV times. Since the numbers of observations are different for the two groups, using the percent of counts in each interval rather than the counts themselves provides a more effective comparison of the two distributions.

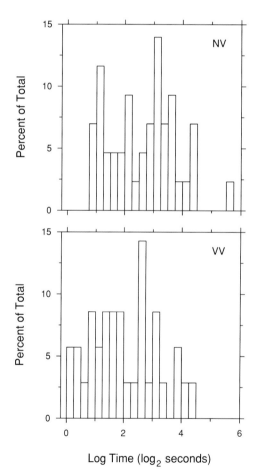

3.9 HISTOGRAM. Each histogram shows the percentage of values in intervals of equal length.

A one-dimensional scatterplot is a reasonable display when the number of observations is not large. In Figure 3.8 we probably have reached the upper limit of the number of values that can be effectively shown without offsetting the plotting symbols in the horizontal direction to avoid overlap. When the number of values is large, or even moderate, the histogram is the better display to use. This is illustrated in Figure 3.10; the histogram shows redshifts of quasars from a catalog compiled by Adelaide Hewitt and Geoffrey Burbidge, two astronomers at the Kitt Peak National Observatory in Tucson, Arizona [59].

It should be remembered that a histogram reduces the information in the data. A measured value, such as a redshift, is itself usually an interval of values because there is limited accuracy in measuring devices and because data are often rounded. When a histogram is made, the interval width of the histogram is generally greater than the data inaccuracy interval, so accuracy is lost. As we decrease the interval width of a histogram, accuracy increases but the appearance becomes more ragged until finally we have what amounts to a one-dimensional scatterplot. In most applications it makes sense to choose the interval width on the basis of what seems like a tolerable loss in the accuracy of the data; no general rules are possible because the tolerable loss depends on the subject matter and the goal of the analysis.

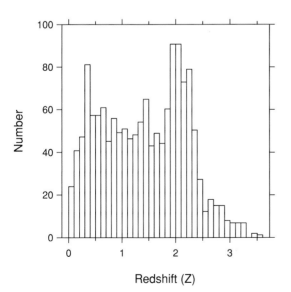

3.10 HISTOGRAM. In most applications it makes sense to choose the interval width on the basis of what seems like a tolerable loss in accuracy of the data. In this example the width is 0.1 units.

One-dimensional scatterplots and histograms certainly do a good job of showing us individual distributions of data sets, but they generally do not provide *comparisons* of distributions that are as incisive as methods that will be described later in this section. Figures 3.8 and 3.9 suggest that the increased prior information given to the VV group reduced viewing times, but the two graphs give us little quantitative information about the magnitude of the difference.

Quantile Plots

Figure 3.11 shows *quantile plots* of the two distributions of stereogram times. An f *quantile* of a distribution is a number, q, such that approximately a fraction f of the values of the distribution is less than or equal to q; f is the *f-value* of q. The *median* is the 0.5 quantile, the *lower quartile* is the 0.25 quantile, and the *upper quartile* is the 0.75 quantile.

Suppose x_1 is the smallest observation in a data set, x_2 is the next to smallest, and so forth up to x_n, which is the largest observation. For example, if the data are

$$5 \quad 1 \quad 9 \quad 3 \quad 14 \quad 9 \quad 7$$

then

$$x_1 = 1 \quad x_2 = 3 \quad x_3 = 5 \quad x_4 = 7 \quad x_5 = 9 \quad x_6 = 9 \quad x_7 = 14 \ .$$

We will take x_i to be the f_i quantile of the data where

$$f_i = \frac{i - 0.5}{n} \ .$$

For the above set of seven values

$$f_1 = (1 - 0.5)/7 = 0.071$$
$$f_2 = (2 - 0.5)/7 = 0.214$$

and so forth to

$$f_7 = (7 - 0.5)/7 = 0.929 \ .$$

On the quantile plot each x_i is graphed against its f-value, f_i.

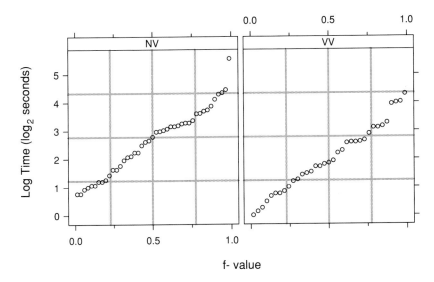

3.11 QUANTILE PLOT. On each panel, the data are graphed against their f-values. The f-value for an observation is very nearly the fraction of the data that is less than or equal to the observation.

Subtracting 0.5 in the formula for the f-value of x_i is a convention in statistical science [16] and arises from the desire to make the definition of the quantile of a set of data as consistent as possible with the concept of the quantile of a theoretical probability distribution, such as the normal. One piece of heuristic reasoning that might satisfy some is the following: Suppose x_i is the result of rounding. When we count how many observations are less than or equal to x_i, we count only 1/2 for x_i itself, because there is a 50-50 chance that the actual value of the observation is less than or equal to x_i, the recorded value. But for quantile plots the subtraction of 0.5 is a trivial issue that has little affect on the visual appearance of the display.

Quantile plots are often more effective for comparing data distributions than one-dimensional scatterplots or histograms because the f_i are shown, which means corresponding quantiles can be compared. For example, Figure 3.11 shows that the median of the NV times is slightly less than $3 \log_2$ seconds; this median value can be compared with that of the VV times, which is about $2 \log_2$ seconds. Comparing quantiles is usually the most informative way to compare two distributions; we will return to this point later.

So far, we have defined quantiles only for the values f_i. In other words, we know only that x_i is the f_i quantile. But for other purposes we will need quantiles with f-values other than f_i. For the example introduced earlier, the x_i and f_i are

i	x_i	f_i
1	1	0.071
2	3	0.214
3	5	0.357
4	7	0.500
5	9	0.643
6	9	0.786
7	14	0.929

Suppose we want the median. One of the x_i happens to be the 0.5 quantile, so we have the value. But suppose we want the lower quartile. The value 0.25 is not equal to one of the f_i.

We can get other quantiles by linearly interpolating and extrapolating the x_i and f_i values. Here is a simple way to do the computation for the f quantile. We want a value of v such that

$$\frac{v - 0.5}{n} = f .$$

Solving for v we get

$$v = nf + 0.5 .$$

If v turns out to be an integer then x_v is the f quantile. However, v will often not be an integer. Let k be the integer part of v and let p be the fractional part; for example, if $v = 10.375$ then $k = 10$ and $p = 0.375$. Suppose for the moment that $k \geq 1$ and $k \leq n - 1$ The f quantile using linear interpolation is

$$(1 - p)x_k + px_{k+1} .$$

If $k = 0$, the quantile is x_1; if $k = n$, the quantile is x_n. Let us apply this to the computation of the 0.25 quantile for the above set of seven values.

$$v = 7 \cdot 0.25 + 0.5 = 2.25 .$$

The 0.25 quantile is

$$0.75\, x_2 + 0.25\, x_3 = 0.75 \cdot 3 + 0.25 \cdot 5 = 3.5 \ .$$

The interpolation rule always leads to a simple result for the median; if n is odd, it is the middle observation, $x_{(n+1)/2}$, and if n is even, it is the average of the two middle observations, $x_{n/2}$ and $x_{n/2+1}$.

Box Plots

It is sometimes enough, in order to convey the salient features of the distribution of a set of data, to show just a summary of the data. One such summary, shown in Figure 3.12, is the Tukey *box plot* [123]. The filled circle encodes the median, a measure of the center, or *location*, of the distribution. The upper and lower ends of the box are the upper and lower quartiles. The distance between these two values, which is the *interquartile range*, is a measure of the *spread* of the distribution. The middle 50% or so of the data lie between the lower and upper quartiles. If the interquartile range is small, the middle data are tightly packed around the median. If the interquartile range is large, the middle data spread out far from the median. The relative distances of the upper and

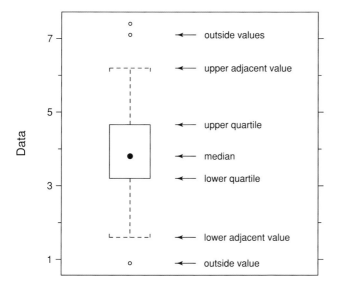

3.12 TUKEY BOX PLOT. A box plot displays a summary of a distribution as illustrated in this figure.

lower quartiles from the median give information about the *shape* of the distribution of the data. If one distance is much bigger than the other, the distribution is *skewed*.

The dashed appendages of the box plot encode the *adjacent values*. Let r be the interquartile range. The upper adjacent value is the largest observation that is less than or equal to the upper quartile plus $1.5r$. The lower adjacent value is the smallest observation that is greater than or equal to the lower quartile minus $1.5r$. Figure 3.13, a quantile plot, demonstrates their computation. The adjacent values also provide summaries of spread and shape, but do so further in the extremes, or *tails*, of the distribution.

Outside values, observations beyond the adjacent values, are graphed individually. Sometimes, the upper adjacent value is the maximum of the data, so there are no outside values in the upper tail; a similar statement holds for the lower tail. Outside values portray behavior in the extreme tails of the distribution, providing further information about spread and shape. If there happen to be outliers — unusually large or small observations — they appear as outside values, so box plots do not sweep outliers under the rug.

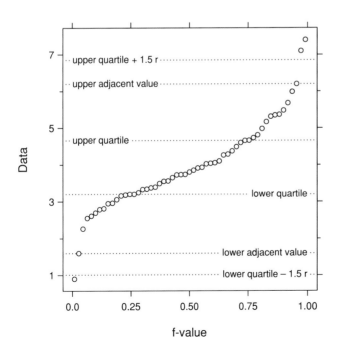

3.13 ADJACENT VALUES. The diagram illustrates the computation of the adjacent values, which are used in the box plot display method.

Box plots provide an effective comparison of distributions. The reason is that we can readily compare the commensurate values — the medians, the upper quartiles, the lower quartiles, and so forth. For example, in Figure 3.14, box plots of the fusion times, we can see easily that the medians of the NV times and VV times differ by roughly one $\log_2$ second, or a factor of 2. Also, box plots can be used even when the number of distributions is not small.

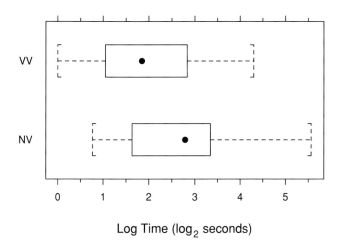

3.14 BOX PLOT. Box plots are an excellent way to compare distributions because they allow us to readily compare commensurate quantities of the distributions. In this example we see the median of the NV times is greater than that for the VV times by about a factor of 2.

In Figure 3.15 ten distributions are compared by box plots. The data on the vertical scale are the payoffs from 254 runnings of the daily New Jersey Pick-It Lottery just after the lottery began. In this game a player picks a three-digit number from 000 to 999. It costs 50 cents to bet on one number. Players who selected the winning number share the prize, which is half of the money bet on that day. Since the drawing of the winning number is random, so that all numbers are equally likely, the best strategy is to pick a number that few other people are likely to pick.

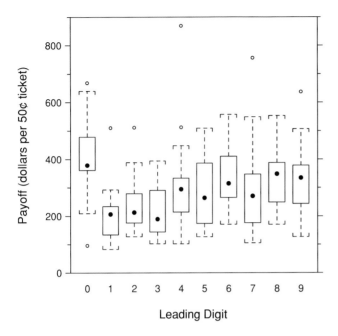

3.15 BOX PLOT. The vertical scale is the payoff of the New Jersey lottery, or numbers game, in which a player picks a three-digit number from 000 to 999. Winners share half of the pot. Each box plot shows the distribution of payoffs for all numbers with a particular leading digit.

The payoffs in Figure 3.15 have been divided into ten groups according to the winning number. The first group, labeled "0", is winning numbers from 000 to 099; the second group is 100 to 199; the third group is 200 to 299; and so forth. Thus the ten box plots give a comparison of the ten distributions of payoffs.

Figure 3.15 has a clear message: the payoffs for numbers starting with zero tend to be high, which means bettors avoid them. One exception to this behavior is a zero-starting number with a payoff around $100, which is nearly the lowest value of all payoffs; in this case the winning number was 000, and it is not surprising that it was a popular one. There is an interesting trend in the remaining nine groups of numbers. The payoffs tend to increase in going from the smaller to the larger numbers, but in a zigzag fashion, suggesting that odd first digits are preferred to even.

If bettors' choices were uniformly distributed over all the numbers, the expected payoff would be $250 (not $500 since the state takes half of the money). However, the graph suggests that by the right choice of a number with a leading 0 we might be able to push the expected payoff above $500, the break-even point. Unfortunately, this is no longer true. Richard Becker and John Chambers showed that as time went along

New Jersey Pick-It players caught on, the distribution of chosen numbers became more nearly uniform, and the maximum payoffs declined and rarely exceeded $500 [5].

Q-Q Plots

The *quantile-quantile plot*, or *q-q plot*, invented by Martin Wilk and Ram Gnanadesikan, satisfies the primary conditions of a great invention; it is both powerful and simple [132].

When distributions are compared, the goal is usually to rank the categories according to how much each has of the variable being measured; for the stereogram times we want to know which group took more time, and for the lottery data we are interested in finding the leading digits that give the highest payoffs. The most effective way to investigate which of two distributions has more is to compare the corresponding quantiles. This was the insightful observation of Wilk and Gnanadesikan. Their method is to simply graph the quantiles of one distribution against the corresponding quantiles of the other distribution. For example, we might graph the median of the first data set against the median of the second data set, the upper quartile of the first against the upper quartile of the second, and so forth.

The left panel of Figure 3.16 is a q-q plot; the two data sets are the scores of males and the scores of females on the verbal SAT test [106]. There were 464,733 people in the males' data set and 497,809 in the females' data set. The highest possible score on the test is 800 and the lowest is 200. The following values are 100 times the f-values of the quantiles of the distributions that are shown on the graph:

1 2 3 4 5 10 20 30 40 50 60 70 80 90 95 96 97 98 99

The point in the lower left corner of the data rectangle is the 0.01 quantile for the males against the 0.01 quantile for the females, and the point in the upper right corner of the data rectangle is the 0.99 quantile for the males against the 0.99 quantile for the females. The right panel of Figure 3.16 uses the Tukey mean-difference plot, discussed in Section 3.2 (pp. 126–132), to give a clearer picture of the differences of the quantiles.

How do we make the q-q plot? Suppose, first, that there is a moderate number of observations in the smaller of the two data sets, say no more than 1000. Let $x_1, \ldots, x_n$ be the first data set, ordered from smallest to largest, and let $y_1, \ldots, y_m$ be the second set of data, also ordered.

Suppose $m = n$. Then y_i and x_i are both $(i - 0.5)/n$ quantiles of their respective data sets, so we would make the q-q plot by graphing y_i against x_i. Thus in the $m = n$ case the graph is quite simple — we just graph the ordered values for one group against the ordered values of the other group.

Suppose $m < n$. Then y_i is the $(i - 0.5)/m$ quantile of the y data, so on the q-q plot we graph y_i against the $(i - 0.5)/m$ quantile of the x data, which typically must be computed by interpolation. Thus in the case of an unequal number of observations in the two data sets, there are as many points on the graph as there are values in the smaller of the two data sets.

The left panel of Figure 3.17 illustrates the unequal case; the display is a q-q plot of the stereogram data: the 43 NV times and 35 VV times. There are 35 points on the panel. For example, the 9th VV time is $y_9 = 1.0 \log_2$ seconds; this is a quantile with f-value 0.243, and it is graphed against the 0.243 quantile of the NV times, which was computed by interpolating the 10th and 11th NV times, y_{10} and y_{11}. The interpolated value is $0.06\, y_{10} + 0.94\, y_{11} = 1.62 \log_2$ seconds.

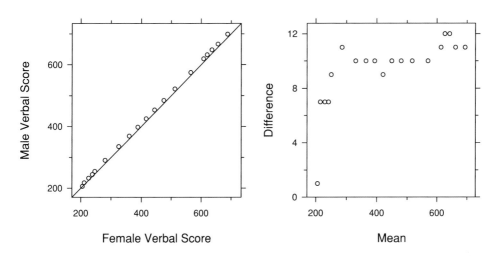

3.16 Q-Q PLOT. The q-q plot, illustrated in the left panel, is a simple but powerful tool for comparing two distributions. Quantiles from one distribution are graphed against corresponding quantiles from the other distribution. The data in this figure are scores of males and females on the verbal SAT test. The right panel is a Tukey mean-difference plot of the values in the left panel. The graph shows that throughout most of the range of the distribution, scores of males are about 10 points higher.

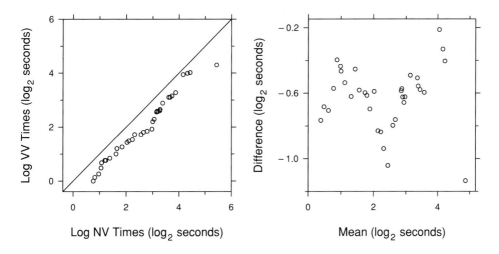

3.17 Q-Q PLOT. In the left panel quantiles of the VV times are graphed against corresponding quantiles of the NV times. The right panel is a Tukey mean-difference plot. Throughout the entire range of the distribution, the NV times are greater than the VV times; the average increase is about 0.6 log base 2 seconds, which is a factor of 1.5.

Suppose the smaller of the two data sets has a large number of values. For example, for the SAT data the smaller group, the males, has 464,899 values. We do not need, of course, to graph 464,899 points, because far fewer points can characterize the differences between the two distributions. In such a case a liberal helping of quantiles, with f-values ranging from close to 0 to close to 1, can be graphed against one another. In many cases, as few as 15 to 25 quantiles can adequately compare the two distributions. As described earlier, this procedure was used for the q-q plot of the SAT scores in Figure 3.16.

The question of which of two distributions has more and by how much is a simple one whose answer can be complicated. The q-q plot, by giving us a detailed comparison of the two distributions, can show whether the answer is simple or complicated, and if complicated, just what the complication is. This will be illustrated by several examples.

Figure 3.16 shows that the way in which the scores of males and females differ is relatively simple. Throughout most of the range of the distribution, the males' quantiles are about 10 points higher than the females' quantiles, but at the very bottom end the difference tapers off. Thus a reasonable summary of the pattern of the points is a line parallel to the line $y = x$ with an equation $y = x + 10$. The comparison of the two distributions can be summarized by the simple statement that the males' scores are about 10 points higher throughout most of the range of the distributions.

Figure 3.18 is a q-q plot of made-up test scores. The pattern is a line through the origin with equation $y = 0.8x$. Now it is not true that the corresponding quantiles differ by a constant amount as they did for the verbal SAT scores; now the high quantiles differ by more than the low ones. But because the general pattern is a line through the origin with slope 0.8, the percentage decrease of the males' scores is a fixed amount. That is, because the males' scores, y, are approximately related to the females' scores, x, by $y = 0.8x$, we have $(y - x)/x = -0.2$, which means the males' scores are approximately 20% lower throughout the range of the distributions.

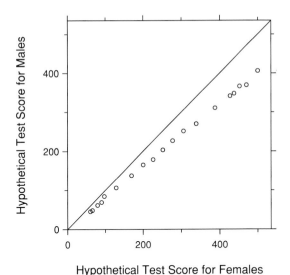

3.18 Q-Q PLOT. The data are hypothetical test scores. Since the points lie close to a line through the origin with slope 0.8, scores of males are about 20% lower throughout most of the range of the distribution.

If we were to take the logarithms of the values in Figure 3.18 the multiplicative pattern would be transformed into an additive pattern like Figure 3.16. In Figure 3.17, logarithms performed such a multiplicative-to-additive transformation for the stereogram times. The general pattern of the points in Figure 3.17 is a line, $y = x + k$, where k is about 0.6 $\log_2$ seconds. Had we graphed the points without taking logarithms the general pattern would have been a line through the origin with slope $2^{0.6} = 1.5$.

Figure 3.19 compares two other sets of hypothetical scores. The pattern of the data is a line with a slope less than 1; the line $y = x$ intersects this pattern at the medians of the distributions. The medians of the two groups are equal, but the distributions differ in a major way: the high scores for the females are higher than the high scores for the males, and the low scores for the males are higher than the low scores for the females. The two distributions are centered at the same place but the females' scores are more spread out.

3.4   Dot Plots

3.22 DOT PLOT. A dot plot shows the fraction of space devoted to graphs for 57 scientific journals. The dot plot is a graphical method for measurements that have labels.

Sometimes, measurements of a quantitative variable are labeled. Figure 3.22 shows an example. The data are from a survey on the amount of use of graphs in 57 scientific publications [24]. For each journal, 50 articles from the period were sampled. The variable graphed in Figure 3.22 is the fraction of space of the 50 articles devoted to graphs (not including captions) and the labels are the journal names. Figure 3.22 is a *dot plot*, a graphical method that was invented to display such labeled data [23].

Figure 3.23 is another dot plot. The data are the ratios of extragalactic to galactic energy in seven frequency bands [89], where energy is measured per unit volume. The frequencies in the seven bands increase in going from the top of the graph to the bottom. In five of the seven bands the galaxies have much higher intensities than the space between galaxies. One of these five bands is visible light; this should come as no surprise since on a clear night on the earth we can see galactic matter in the form of stars (or light reflected from a star by our moon) and only blackness in between. For microwaves and x-rays there is much more energy coming from outside the galaxies. The extragalactic microwave radiation, discovered by Nobel prize winners Arno Penzias and Robert Wilson of AT&T Bell Laboratories in 1965 [103], has an explanation: it is the remnant of the big bang that gave our universe its start. But the extragalactic x-ray radiation remains a mystery whose solution might also tell us something fundamental about the structure of the universe.

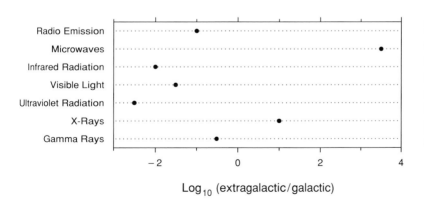

3.23 DOT PLOT. The dot plot is a far more effective display than a number of other methods for displaying labeled data such as pie charts, bar charts, and divided bar charts.

Log_{10} (extragalactic/galactic)

The encoding scheme in Figure 3.35 is different geometric shapes; the visual assembly appears somewhat better than for the letters in Figure 3.34. In Figure 3.36 four types of circle fill are used to encode the categories. Theoretical and experimental evidence from the field of visual perception suggests that different methods of fill should provide effective assembly [35]. In fact, Figure 3.36 appears to provide better assembly than the other two figures.

Figure 3.36 shows two interesting phenomena: social science journals and mathematical science journals tend to use graphs less than the other two categories, and the biological science journals tend to have more in the figure captions. The second phenomenon is probably due to the tendency in biological journals to put experimental procedures in figure captions.

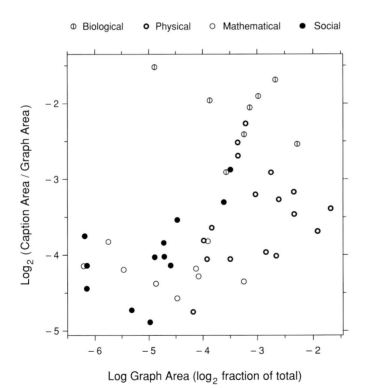

3.36 SUPERPOSED SYMBOLS. The data of Figure 3.34 are graphed with the categories encoded by circles with different methods of fill. This provides the best visual assembly of the methods shown in Figures 3.34 to 3.36.

The encoding scheme in Figure 3.36 works well if there is not much overlap of the plotting symbols. When there is overlap, the solid portions of the symbols can form uninterpretable blobs. In such a case we must attempt to use symbols that provide effective visual assembly, subject to the constraint that the symbols tolerate overlap. The constraint seems to restrict us to symbols consisting of curves and lines, with no solid parts, and with a minimum of ink. One encoding scheme that does quite well is shown in Figure 3.37, a graph of brain weights and body weights for four categories of animals [41]. The symbols used are called *texture symbols* since they were chosen based on research in the visual perception of textures [25]. This will be discussed in Section 4.4 (pp. 234–239).

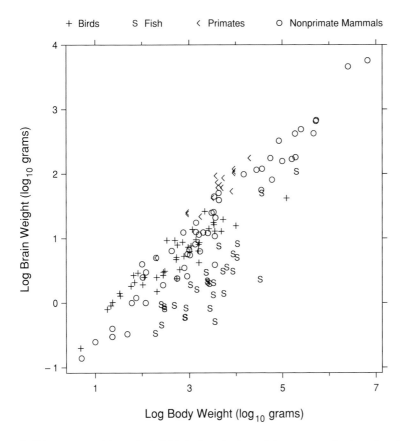

3.37 SUPERPOSED SYMBOLS. Log brain weights are graphed against log body weights for four categories of animals. The texture plotting symbols used on this graph to encode the animal category provide good visual assembly and can tolerate overlap.

3.6   Visual Reference Grids

Sometimes the only solution for effective assembly of different data sets is to give up superposition and use juxtaposition of two or more panels. This is illustrated in Figure 3.41, which shows model predictions of temperature in the Northern Hemisphere following different types of nuclear exchanges [125]. The temperatures following major exchanges drop precipitously due to soot from conflagrations of cities and forests and due to dust from soil and vaporization of earth and rock. The soot and dust substantially reduce radiation from the sun which, in turn, causes the temperature to drop.

The temperatures are computed from physical models that describe the creation of particles, the production of radiation, convection, and a script for the nuclear war. The panels in Figure 3.41 are different exchange scenarios:

Code	Description
10 gt	10 gt exchange.
5 gt	5 gt exchange.
5 gt air	5 gt airburst in which all weapons are detonated above ground.
5 gt dust	5 gt exchange with only the effects of dust included, but not fires.
3 gt	3 gt exchange.
3 gt silo	3 gt exchange aimed only at missile silos.
1 gt	1 gt exchange.
0.1 gt city	0.1 gt exchange aimed only at major cities.

Figure 3.41 uses a graphical method that greatly improves our ability to compare the values on the different panels — a *visual reference grid*, the vertical and horizontal lines in gray. Their purpose is not to enhance table look-up; the tick marks are sufficient for this task. Rather, their purpose is to enhance the comparison of patterns, or gestalts, on different panels. By providing a common visual reference, the grids enhance our comparison of the relative locations of features on different panels. The reasons for the improvement are given in Section 4.5 (pp. 240–243).

Figure 3.41 does a good job of displaying the temperature profiles. The major exchanges result in a rapid drop to around −25°C and then a slow recovery lasting many months. The *0.1 gt city* attack has such a strong effect because of the tremendous concentration of combustible materials in urban areas.

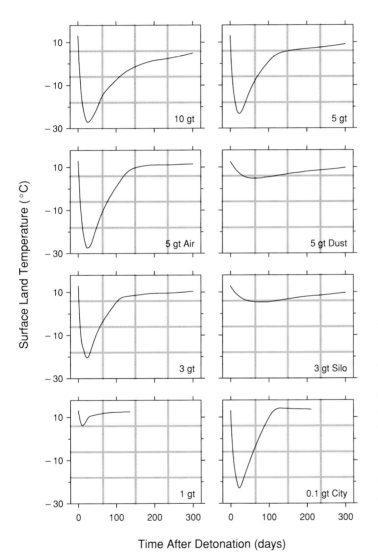

3.41 JUXTAPOSITION. Each curve shows averaged Northern Hemisphere temperature following a nuclear war. The scenarios of the war are different for different panels. On this graph the different data sets are juxtaposed. Comparisons of the curves are enhanced by the visual reference grid. The curves are banked to 45°.

3.7 Loess

Figure 3.42 graphs data from an experiment on 144 hamsters [85]. The least-squares fit of a line to the data is also shown on the display. The two measured variables are hamster lifetime and the fraction of lifetime spent hibernating. The data were also graphed in Section 2.2 (pp. 25–54). The objective of the experiment was to see how lifetime depends on hibernation. Thus lifetime is a response and hibernation is a factor.

Figure 3.42 shows that as hibernation increases, lifetime tends to increase. One hypothesis suggested by this behavior is that hamster DNA parcels out a fixed amount of nonhibernation hours; a hamster gets only so much awake time, and if it hibernates longer, it lives longer by the same amount, but otherwise there is no effect on lifetime. Suppose ℓ is the lifetime and f is the fraction of lifetime spent hibernating. If the hypothesis is true then $(1 - f)\ell$, the amount of time spent not hibernating, does not depend on $f\ell$, the amount of time spent hibernating.

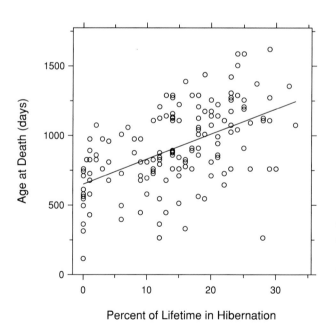

3.42 FACTOR-RESPONSE DATA. Age at death is graphed against fraction of lifetime spent hibernating for 144 hamsters. The goal is to study how hibernation depends on lifetime so lifetime is the response and hibernation is the factor.

Figure 3.43 is a graph of time spent not hibernating against time spent hibernating. It shows that, overall, the hypothesis is false; increased hibernation time results in increased nonhibernation time. But how would we describe the dependence? Is there a linear or nonlinear dependence? With a graph of just the (x_i, y_i) values it is hard to answer these questions.

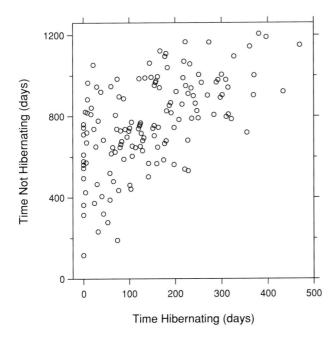

3.43 FACTOR-RESPONSE DATA. The total time spent not hibernating is graphed against the time spent hibernating for the 144 hamsters. There appears to be a dependence of y on x but it is difficult to assess the nature of the dependence from the graph.

In Figure 3.44 a smooth curve has been added to the hamster scatterplot. The curve was produced by a smoothing procedure called *locally weighted regression* [22,27,28]. The name of the procedure is often shortened to *lowess*, or *loess*. Loess produces smoothed values at any desired collection of values along the x scale. Then a curve is rendered by connecting successive values from left to right by line segments. In Figure 3.44 the loess fit was computed at 100 equally-spaced values along the horizontal scale, beginning at the minimum value of x_i and ending at the maximum. The loess method of fitting will be described shortly.

The purpose of the loess curve is to summarize the *middle* of the distribution of y for each value of x. Statistical scientists call this a *regression curve*, a misnomer since there is nothing regressive about it.

The loess curve shows that there is some truth to the hypothesis stated earlier. While there is, overall, an increase in nonhibernation lifetime as hibernation increases, the response is in fact constant until the amount of hibernation is above 100 days. From 100 days and above, the effect is nearly linear and the slope is about 1, so each minute spent hibernating beyond 100 days produces on the average about one extra minute of nonhibernation lifetime. We have been assuming that there is a causal mechanism, but this is reasonable in view of biological information [85].

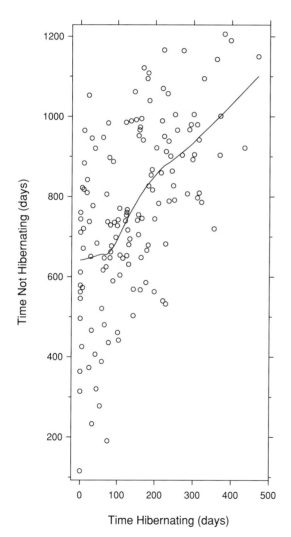

3.44 LOESS. The smooth curve, which was computed by a procedure called loess, summarizes how y depends on x. The loess smoothing parameter is $\alpha = 0.5$. The line segments that make up the curve are banked to $45°$.

Using Loess

Fitting a loess curve requires choosing a smoothness parameter α, a positive number less than or equal to 1. As α increases, the smooth curve becomes smoother. In Figure 3.44 the value of α is 0.5 and in Figure 3.45 it is 0.25. Loess is very computing intensive, but there is a fast, efficient computer program that carries it out [32].

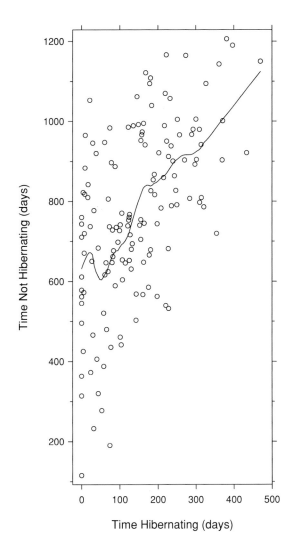

3.45 LOESS. The smoothness of the loess curve depends on a smoothness parameter, α, a positive number less than or equal to 1. As α increases the curve becomes smoother. In Figure 3.44, α = 0.5 and in this figure, α = 0.25. The aspect ratio of this display is the same as that of Figure 3.44 to facilitate comparison of the two curves.

Choosing α requires some judgment for each application. In most applications an α that works well is usually between 0.25 and 1. The goal is to make α as large as possible to make the curve as smooth as possible, without distorting the underlying pattern in the data. Residuals, useful in so many situations, can help in choosing α.

Figure 3.46 is a graph of the air pollutant ozone against wind speed for 111 days in New York City from May 1 to September 30 of one year. The data were displayed in Section 1.3 (pp. 16–21). From this graph we can see that the general pattern is for ozone to decrease as wind speed increases because of the increased ventilation of air pollution that higher wind speeds bring. However, it is difficult to see more precise aspects of the pattern, for example, whether there is a linear or nonlinear decrease.

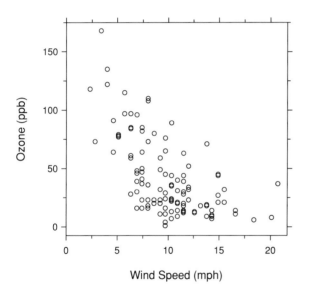

3.46 FACTOR-RESPONSE DATA. The data are daily measurements of ozone and wind speed for 111 days. It is difficult to see the nature of the dependence of ozone on wind speed.

The top panel of Figure 3.47, which has a loess curve with $\alpha = 0.8$, suggests the decrease is nonlinear. But how do we know the loess curve is not distorting the pattern? Since we cannot discern easily the pattern when a loess curve is absent we cannot expect to assess easily how well loess is doing. The solution is to compute a value of the curve, $\widehat{y}_i$, at x_i, graph the residuals $y_i - \widehat{y}_i$ against x_i, add a loess smoothing to this graph of residuals, and see if there is an effect. This is illustrated in the bottom panel of Figure 3.47. The loess curve on the residual graph suggests that there is some dependence of the residuals on x_i. This should not happen; the curve should be nearly a horizontal line since the residuals should be variation in y_i not explainable by x_i. The problem is that the loess smoothing in the top panel has missed part of the pattern because α is too large, and this missed part has gone into the residuals.

In Figure 3.48, α has been reduced to 0.5. The curve on the graph of the residuals is now reasonably close to a horizontal line, so the amount of smoothing for the curve in the top panel is not too great.

This method of graphing and smoothing residuals is a one-sided test: it can show us when α is too large but sets off no alarm when α is too small. One way to keep α from being too small is to increase it to the point where the residual graph just begins to show a pattern, and then use a slightly smaller value of α.

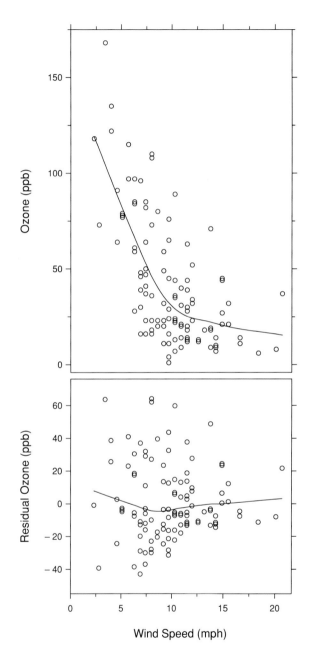

3.47 CHECKING LOESS. In the top panel the graph from Figure 3.46 now has a loess curve with $\alpha = 0.8$. The curve is banked to 45°. It is difficult to assess visually whether loess is correctly depicting the dependence. On the bottom panel the residuals are graphed against wind speed and a loess curve is superposed; for the curve on this display, $\alpha = 0.8$. The loess curve suggests there is a small dependence of the residuals on wind speed, which means α is too large in the smoothing of the top panel.

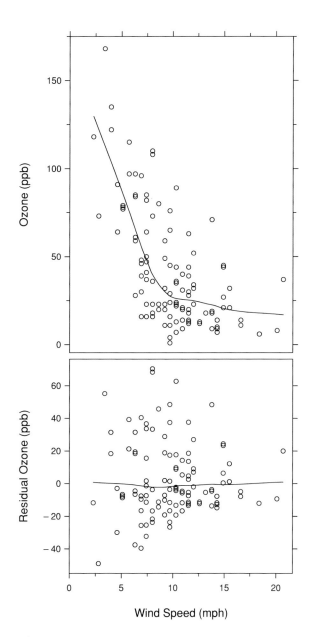

3.48 CHECKING LOESS. On the top panel the value of α for loess has been reduced to 0.5 since Figure 3.47 suggests $\alpha = 0.8$ is too large. The curve is banked to 45°. The bottom panel shows no dependence of the residuals on wind speed, which suggests the loess curve with $\alpha = 0.5$ is not distorting the underlying pattern. For the loess curve on the bottom panel, $\alpha = 0.8$.

The same operations can be carried out for any other value of x. Figure 3.50 shows them at $x = 27$, which happens to be the value of the largest x_i. The right boundary of the strip does not appear in the top panels because it is beyond the right extreme of the horizontal scale line.

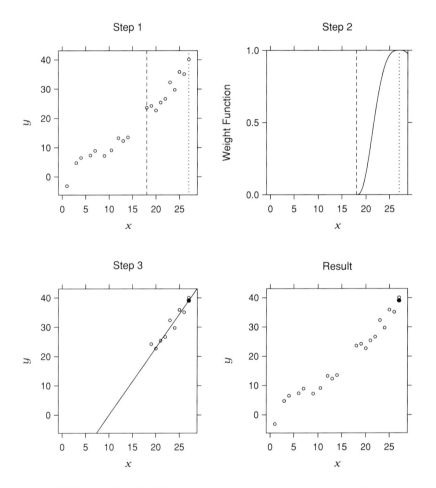

3.50 HOW LOESS WORKS. The computation of the initial loess fit value at $x = 27$ is illustrated.

The next stage of the fitting provides protection against *outliers* in the data; an outlier is a point, (x_i, y_i), with an unusually large or small value of y_i compared with other points in a vertical strip around x_i. The left panel of Figure 3.51 shows an example of data with an outlier. The unfilled circles are the data and one point, (x_{11}, y_{11}), has a y value that is much larger than the y values of points whose x values are close to x_{11}. The smooth curve is the initial loess fit; the outlier has distorted the fit in the neighborhood of x_{11} so that the general pattern of the data is no longer described.

In the first loess robustness iteration, residuals are computed from the initial fit, and *robustness weights*, r_i, are assigned to the observations (x_i, y_i) based on the magnitudes of the residuals. If a residual is zero, the weight is one; as the absolute values of the residuals increase, the weights decrease to zero. So an outlier, which tends to have a large residual, will tend to have a small weight. Now the loess fitting is altered by including the r_i. For the altered fitting method, the weight given to x_i for the fit at x is the neighborhood weight $w_i(x)$ times the robustness weight r_i. Thus (x_i, y_i) has a small weight if either x_i is far from x or r_i is large. Using this altered fitting, a new loess fit is computed. This completes the first robustness iteration.

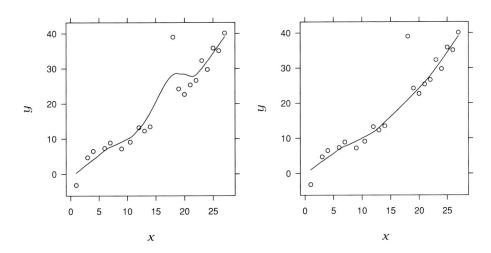

3.51 HOW LOESS WORKS. Loess employs robustness iterations that prevent outliers from distorting the fit. (Left panel) The open circles are the points of the graph; there is one outlier between $x = 15$ and $x = 20$. The initial loess curve has been distorted in the neighborhood of the outlier. (Right panel) The graphed curve is the fit after four robustness iterations. Now the fit follows the general pattern of the data.

Each successive robustness iteration proceeds in the same manner as the first. The residuals from the previous step are computed, and then the robustness weights are computed; the next step incorporates the new weights. We will use four robustness iterations; in most applications there is little change after the fourth. This last iteration produces final robust weights that are used to compute the final loess curve at any set of points. For the data in Figure 3.51 the graphed curve in the right panel is the final fit. It is displayed by evaluating it at a grid of 100 equally spaced values from the minimum value of the x_i to the maximum, and then connecting these evaluated curve points by line segments.

The final fit in Figure 3.51 is doing its job properly; it describes the behavior of the majority of the data.

3.8   Time Series

A *time series* is a set of measurements of a variable through time. Figure 3.52 shows an example. The data are yearly values, from 1868 to 1967, of the aa index, which measures the magnitude of fluctuations in the earth's magnetic field [92]. The index is the average of measurements of geomagnetic fluctuations at observatories in Australia and England that are roughly antipodal: at opposite ends of an earth diameter. Figure 3.52 shows there has been an increase in the overall level of the aa index from 1900 to 1967. The solar wind causes fluctuations in the earth's magnetic field, so the increase in the index suggests that the solar wind has increased during this century [48]. Figure 3.52 also shows the aa index has cycles with an average period of about 11 years. This is the same as the sunspot cycle; increased sunspots are associated with increased solar activity and therefore an increased solar wind, but interestingly, the sunspots do not show an increase in their overall level, as the aa index does.

A time series is a special case of the broader category of factor-response data. For a time series, time is the factor. One important property of most time series is that for each time point of the data there is only a single value of the response. And time series have different frequency components of variation. There can be long-term trends in the data, there can be very rapid oscillations, and there can be intermediate-term oscillations. These special properties invite special graphical methods.

Four Graphical Methods

There are many ways to graph a time series. Figure 3.52 is a *connected symbol plot* since symbols together with lines connecting successive points are used. Figure 3.53 is a *symbol plot* because just the symbols are used, and Figure 3.54 is a *connected plot* because just the lines are used. Figure 3.55 is a *vertical line plot*.

Each of these four methods of graphing a time series has its data sets for which it provides the best portrayal. For the aa data the best one is the connected symbol plot. The symbol plot does not give a clear portrayal of the 11-year cycles because we cannot perceive the order of the series over short time periods of several years. On the connected plot the individual data points are not unambiguously portrayed. For example, it is clear that there is an unusual peak in the observations around 1930, but it is hard to decide if the peak is a single outlier for one year or is supported by a rise and fall of a few values. On the connected symbol plot, and the other graphs, it is clear that the peak consists of one value. On the vertical line plot there is an unfortunate asymmetry. The peaks of the 11-year cycle stand out more clearly than the troughs. There is also a disconcerting visual phenomenon; our visual system cannot simultaneously perceive the peaks and the troughs.

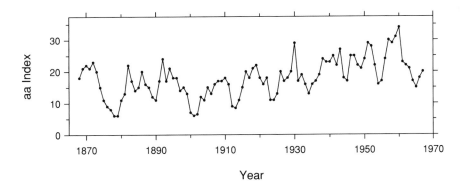

3.52 CONNECTED SYMBOL PLOT. The time series shown on the graph is the yearly average of the aa index: measurements of the magnitudes of fluctuations in the earth's magnetic field. A connected symbol plot, which allows us to see the individual data points and the ordering through time, reveals an 11-year cycle and a trend from 1900 to 1967. The aspect ratio was chosen by eye to approximately bank the underlying pattern of the 11-year cycles to 45°.

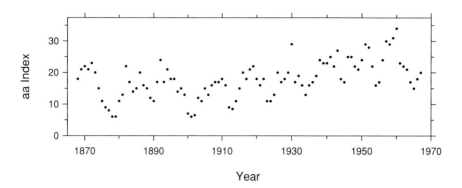

3.53 SYMBOL PLOT. This symbol plot does not display the 11-year cycle effectively.

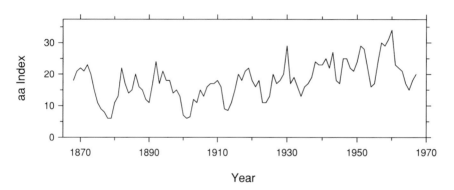

3.54 CONNECTED PLOT. This connected plot does not reveal the positions of the aa measurements.

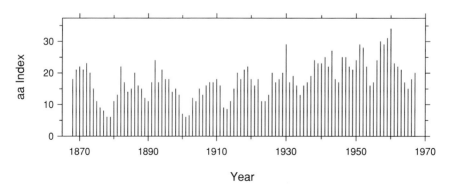

3.55 VERTICAL LINE PLOT. On this vertical line plot the peaks stand out more clearly than the troughs.

A symbol plot of a time series is appropriate if we want to study the long-term trend, that is, the low frequency behavior. In such a case it is not necessary to perceive the exact time order over short time intervals. Figure 3.56 is an example. The data are the ozone concentrations graphed earlier in Figure 3.46, but now logs have been taken and log concentration is graphed against time. One very low ozone value, an outlier on the log scale, has been omitted. In this example the day-to-day movement of ozone is less interesting than the trend, so the symbol plot is used. A loess curve with $\alpha = 0.5$ is superposed to help us see the trend.

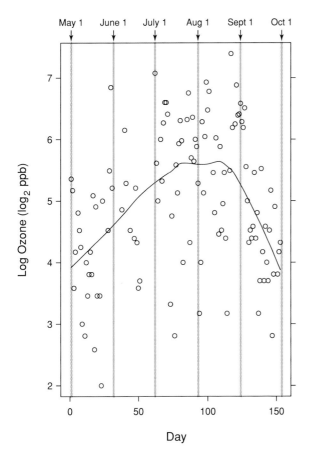

3.56 SYMBOL PLOT. A symbol plot is appropriate for a time series when the goal is to study the long-term trend in the series, but not high frequency behavior. On this symbol plot a loess curve with $\alpha = 0.5$ is superposed to help assess the trend. The curve is banked to 45°.

A connected plot is appropriate when the time series is smooth, so that perceiving individual values is not important. A vertical line plot is appropriate when it is important to see individual values, when we need to see short-term fluctuations, and when the time series has a large number of values; the use of vertical lines allows us to pack the series tightly along the horizontal scale. The vertical line plot, however, usually works best when the vertical lines emanate from a horizontal line through the center of the data and when there are no long-term trends in the data. The connected plot and the vertical line plot are illustrated in Figure 3.57, which shows atmospheric CO_2 concentrations and four frequency components of variation that were discussed in detail in Section 1.1 (pp. 6–9). A connected plot is used for the top four panels because the data are smooth and seeing individual values was not judged important. A vertical line plot, emanating from zero, is used for the bottom panel because it is important in this application to see the individual monthly values and to assess behavior over short time periods, and because the time series is long.

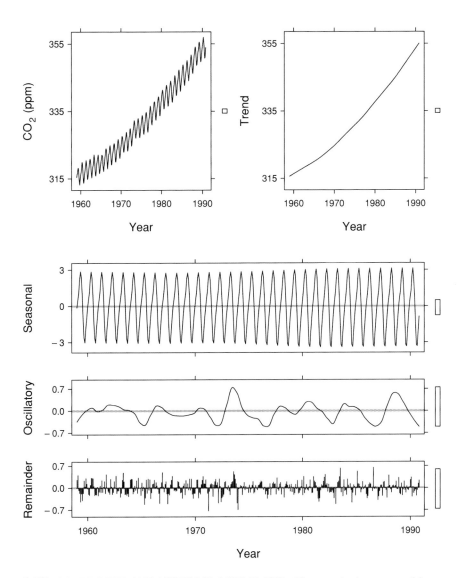

3.57 CONNECTED AND VERTICAL LINE PLOTS. The graph shows monthly average CO_2 concentrations from Mauna Loa and four components of variation. Connected plots are used in the top four panels because it is not important to see individual values and because the four time series are smooth. A vertical line plot is used in the bottom panel since it is important to see individual values and to assess behavior over short periods of time and since the series has many values.

Cycle Plots

Figure 3.58 shows a *cycle plot*, a graphical method that was invented to study the behavior of a seasonal time series [38]. The data in Figure 3.58 are the seasonal component of the CO_2 series in Figure 3.57. In this example it is important to study how the individual monthly subseries are changing through time; for example, we want to analyze the behavior of the January values through time. We cannot make a graphical assessment from Figure 3.57 since it is not possible to focus on the values for a particular month; the graphical method in Figure 3.58 makes it possible.

In the cycle plot of Figure 3.58, the January values of the seasonal component are graphed for successive years, then the February values are graphed, and so forth. For each monthly subseries the mean of the values is portrayed by a horizontal line. The graph allows an assessment of the overall pattern of the seasonal, as portrayed by the horizontal mean lines, and also of the behavior of each monthly subseries. Since all of the monthly subseries are on the same graph we can readily see whether the change in any subseries is large or small compared with the overall pattern of the seasonal component.

Figure 3.58 shows interesting features. The first is the overall seasonal pattern, with a May maximum and an October minimum. This pattern has long been recognized and is due to the earth's vegetation, as discussed in Section 1.1 (pp. 6–9). The second feature is the patterns in the individual monthly subseries. For months near the yearly maximum, the subseries tend to be increasing rapidly although the overall increases are small compared with the seasonal amplitude; the biggest increases occur for April and May. Near the yearly minimum, cycle subseries tend to be decreasing; the biggest decreases are for September and October. The net effect is an increase in the amplitudes of the seasonal component.

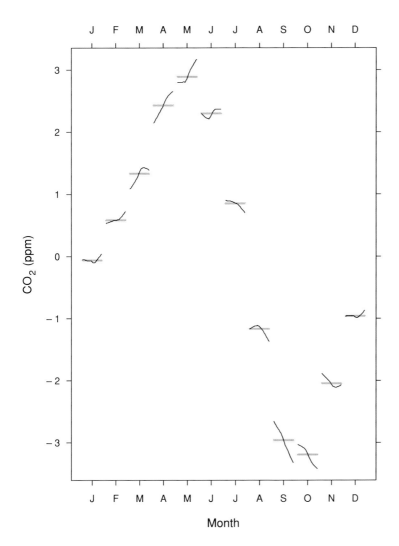

3.58 CYCLE PLOT. The seasonal component from Figure 3.57 is graphed. First the January values are graphed for successive years, then the February values, and so forth. For each monthly subseries the mean of the values is portrayed by a horizontal line.

Cut-and-Stack Plots

Banking to 45° is critical to graphing time series. Examples in Section 2.4 (pp. 66-79) attest to this. But one problem frequently arises — the aspect ratio that banks the local segments of a time series to 45° is too small. The solution must be either a sacrificing of some aspect of the judgment of rate of change or an alternative display method. *Cut-and-stack* is a one such alternative.

Spahr Webb and Charles S. Cox of the Scripps Institution of Oceanography measured pressure fluctuations on the seafloor [131]. One data set, gathered off the coast of California in the U.S. at a depth of 1.6 km, consists of 14,336 pressure measurements made at times spaced 0.25 sec apart. In this case, the aspect ratio that results from banking the local segments is 0.0019 vcm/hcm. Thus, using this value, a graph just 1 cm high must be 5.26 m wide, which is clearly impractical. For any stable time series that has no persistent long-term trend, the aspect ratio that arises from banking the local segments to 45° tends toward zero as the number of observations increases. Thus the small aspect ratio for the pressure data is to be expected.

The solution, shown in Figure 3.61, is to cut and stack. Time increases as we move from left to right and top to bottom. To pack the panels in as tightly as possible, there is just a single horizontal scale that shows the number of seconds from the first measurement on each panel. If we spliced the 19 panels back together to form a continuous trace, the aspect ratio would be 0.0019 vcm/hcm; if we superposed the 19 panels, the single data rectangle would have a shape of 19×0.0019 vcm/hcm = 0.036 vcm/hcm.

Substantial structure is revealed by Figure 3.61. There are cycles with an average period of about 5-6 sec. The authors identify one source of this variation: sea surface swells, probably caused by a distant storm. The graph, however, shows something interesting. Periodically, the cycles break up, lose their amplitude, and become ragged, but then reform again. One possibility is that there are two narrow-band signals with nearly-equal periods; when they are in phase, the amplitude of the waveform is large, and when they go out of phase, the amplitude decreases and the wave form nearly disappears. Using the 45° banking together with the cut-and-stack method has enhanced our ability to perceive this phenomenon.

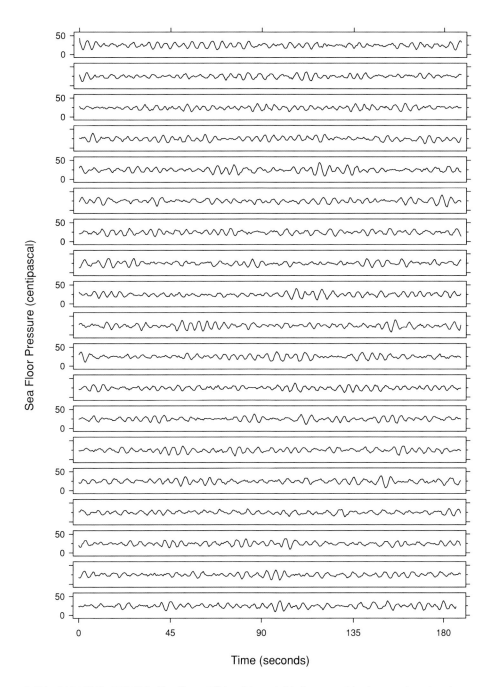

3.61 CUT-AND-STACK. To allow 45° banking of this long, stable time series, the data have been cut and stacked. Time increases from left to right and top to bottom.

The important idea of the scatterplot matrix is to arrange the graphs in a matrix with shared scales. An example is shown in Figure 3.63. There are four variables: wind speed, temperature, solar radiation, and concentrations of the air pollutant, ozone. The data, from a study of the dependence of ozone on meteorological conditions, are measurements of the four variables on 111 days from May to September of one year at sites in the New York City metropolitan region [13]. There is one measurement of each variable on each day; so the data consist of 111 points in a four-dimensional space. The details of the measurements are the following: solar radiation is the amount from 0800 to 1200 in the

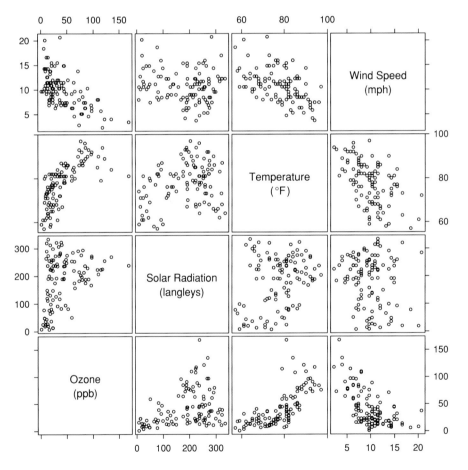

3.63 SCATTERPLOT MATRIX. The data are measurements of ozone, solar radiation, temperature, and wind speed on 111 days. Thus the measurements are 111 points in a four-dimensional space. The graphical method in this figure is a scatterplot matrix: all pairwise scatterplots of the variables are aligned into a matrix with shared scales.

frequency band 4000-7700Å; wind speed is the average of values at 0700 and 1000; temperature is the daily maximum; and ozone is the average of hourly values from 1300 to 1500.

Each panel of the matrix is a scatterplot of one variable against another. For the three graphs in the bottom row of Figure 3.63, the vertical scale is ozone, and the three horizontal scales are solar radiation, temperature, and wind speed. So the graph in position $(2, 1)$ in the matrix — that is, the second column from the left and the first row from the bottom — is a scatterplot of ozone against solar radiation; position $(3, 1)$ is a scatterplot of ozone against temperature; position $(4, 1)$ is a scatterplot of ozone against wind speed.

The upper left triangle of the scatterplot matrix has all of the $k(k - 1)/2$ pairs of scatterplots, and so does the lower right triangle; thus altogether there are $k(k - 1)$ panels and each pair of variables is graphed twice. For example, in Figure 3.63 the $(3, 2)$ panel is a graph of solar radiation on the vertical scale against temperature on the horizontal scale, and the $(2, 3)$ panel has the same variables but with the scales interchanged.

The most important feature of the scatterplot matrix is that we can visually scan a row, or a column, and see one variable graphed against all others with the three scales for the one variable lined up along the horizontal, or the vertical. This is the reason, despite the redundancy, for including both the upper and lower triangles in the matrix. Suppose that in Figure 3.63 only the upper left triangle were present. To see temperature against everything else we would have to scan the first two graphs in the temperature row and then turn the corner to see wind speed against temperature; the three temperature scales would not be lined up, which would make visual assessment more difficult.

Space and resolution quickly become a problem with the scatterplot matrix; the method of construction in Figure 3.63 reduces the problem somewhat. The labels of the variables are inside the boxes along the diagonal so that the graph can expand as much as possible. The tick mark labels for the horizontal scales, as well as for the vertical scales, alternate sides so that labels for successive scales do not interfere with one another. And the panels have been squeezed tightly together, allowing just enough space to provide visual separation.

3.10   Coplots of Scattered Data

The concept of *conditioning* is a fundamental one that forms the basis of a number of graphical methods developed in the past [112,124,134]. And it forms the basis for the *conditioning plot*, or *coplot*, a particularly powerful graphical method for studying how a response variable depends on two or more factor variables. Here, we will show how the coplot is used to graph a response against one factor given another, but the method can also be used to graph a response against a factor given any number of factors [26].

The Coplot Display Method

Figure 3.65, a scatterplot matrix, shows data from an industrial experiment in which thirty rubber specimens were rubbed by an abrasive material [44]. Measurements of three variables — abrasion loss, hardness, and tensile strength — were made for each specimen. Abrasion loss is the amount of material abraded from a specimen per unit of energy expended in the rubbing; tensile strength is the force per unit of cross-sectional area required to break a specimen; and hardness is the rebound height of a steel indenter dropped onto a specimen. The goal is to determine the dependence of abrasion loss on tensile strength and hardness; thus abrasion loss is a response, and hardness and tensile strength are factors.

The hardnesses of the rubber specimens range from 45 °Shore to 89 °Shore. Consider those specimens whose hardnesses lie in the range 45 °Shore to 62 °Shore. There are nine such specimens; their data are displayed in Figure 3.65 by the "+" plotting symbols. Geometrically, we have sliced through the three-dimensional space of the data with two planes that intersect the h scale perpendicularly at 45 °Shore and 62 °Shore, and have selected the specimens that lie between the two planes. On the $(2,3)$ panel of Figure 3.65, the "+" symbols show how abrasion loss depends on tensile strength conditional on hardness lying between 45 °Shore to 62 °Shore. There is a nonlinear conditional dependence.

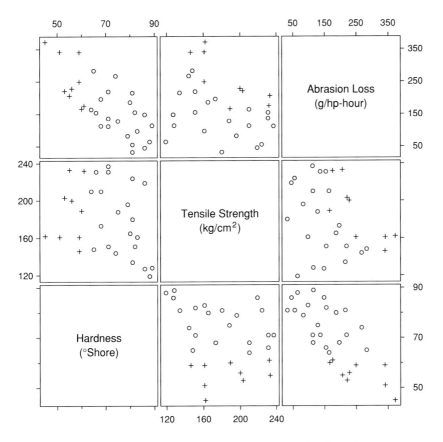

3.65 CONDITIONING. A scatterplot matrix displays trivariate data: measurements of abrasion loss, hardness, and tensile strength for 30 rubber specimens. The "+" plotting symbols encode the data for those specimens with hardness less than 62 °Shore.

The display method of the coplot presents conditional dependence in a visually efficient way. Figure 3.66 illustrates the method using the rubber data. The panel at the top is the *given panel*; the panels below are the *dependence panels*. Each rectangle on the given panel specifies an interval of values of hardness. On a corresponding dependence panel, abrasion loss is graphed against tensile strength for those observations whose values of hardness lie in the interval; a loess curve has been added to the panel. If we start at the (1, 1) dependence panel, the leftmost panel in the bottom row, and move from left to right in the row, then from left to right in the next row, and so forth, the corresponding intervals of the given panel proceed from left to right and from bottom to top in the same fashion.

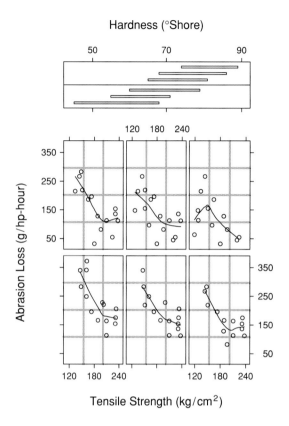

3.66 COPLOT. A coplot graphs abrasion loss against tensile strength given hardness. The smoothing parameter of the six loess curves is $\alpha = 3/4$. The collection of line segments that make up the curves are banked to 45°.

Choosing Coplot Intervals

Coplot intervals must be chosen to compromise between two competing criteria — number of points and resolution. On the one side, their lengths must be sufficiently great that the dependence panels have enough points for effects to be seen; if there are too few points on a dependence panel, noise in the data typically prevents points from coalescing into a meaningful pattern. On the other side, the lengths must be small enough to maintain reasonable resolution; if a conditioning interval is too big, there is a risk of a distorted view if the nature of the dependence changes dramatically as the value of the conditioning factor changes within the interval.

The intervals in Figure 3.66 are the result of using the *equal-count algorithm* [26]. In using the algorithm, we specify the number of intervals and the target fraction of measurements shared by successive intervals. For Figure 3.66, the number of intervals is 6 and the target fraction is 3/4. The algorithm takes the specification and selects intervals to make the numbers of measurements in the intervals as nearly constant as possible, and to make the fraction of measurements shared by each pair of successive intervals as nearly equal to the target fraction as possible. The lower boundary of the lowest interval is the minimum value of the measurements, and the upper boundary of the highest interval is the maximum value of the measurements. The algorithm does its best, but achieving equality is typically not possible. For example, for the intervals in Figure 3.66, the number of measurements in the six intervals ranges from 13 to 16.

The Structure of the Data

Figure 3.66 shows a wealth of information about the dependence of abrasion loss on tensile strength. Except for panel $(3, 2)$, each conditioning on hardness has a nonlinear pattern: a broken-line, or hockey-stick, function. Below 180 kg/cm^2, the pattern is linear; above this value, it is also linear, but with a different slope. On the five panels, the slopes below the breakpoint are negative and nearly equal. Above the breakpoint, the five slopes are nearly equal to zero. In other words, the patterns shift up and down, but do not appear to change otherwise by a significant amount. This suggests that for the most part there is no *interaction* between the two factors; the effect of tensile strength on abrasion loss is the same for most values of hardness. But Panel $(3, 2)$ shows a major departure from the hockey-stick pattern. As tensile strength decreases, the handle of the stick begins to form but then, suddenly, for the lowest three values of tensile strength, the pattern turns precipitously downward.

Figure 3.67 conditions on tensile strength; abrasion loss is graphed against hardness for six intervals of tensile strength chosen, again, using the equal-count algorithm with a target fraction of overlap equal to 3/4. For each conditioning on tensile strength, the dependence of abrasion loss on hardness has, for the most part, a linear pattern. Furthermore, the patterns have roughly the same slope and change only in the intercepts. This supports the observation in Figure 3.66 that, for the most part, there is little or no interaction between hardness and tensile strength. And again, there is a departure from the overall pattern for a small number of points. In panel $(1, 1)$, the observations with the three or so largest values of hardness drop well below the linear pattern established by the other observations. The scatterplot matrix in Figure 3.65 shows that the three observations with the smallest values of tensile strength take on the three largest values of hardness. Thus the aberrant behavior on the two coplots is caused by the same three observations, which sit by themselves in a corner of the factor space.

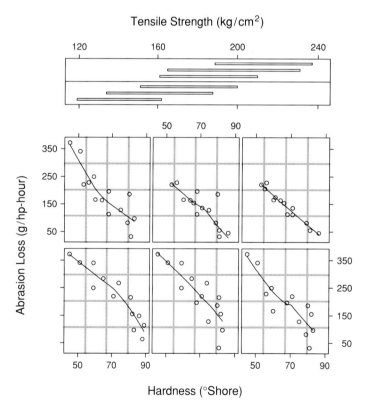

3.67 COPLOT. A coplot graphs abrasion loss against hardness given tensile strength. The smoothing parameter of the six loess curves is $\alpha = 3/4$. The collection of line segments that make up the curves are banked to $45°$.

3.11   Coplots of Surfaces

Coplots can also be used to display surfaces: response functions of two or more factor variables. Here, we will show how the coplot is used to graph a function of two variables, but the method can also be used to graph a function of any number of variables [26].

Figure 3.68 is a coplot of a function, $g(C, E)$. The function arose from an investigation that studied exhaust from an experimental one-cylinder engine fueled by ethanol [11]. The function value is the concentration of the oxides of nitrogen, NO_x, in the exhaust, normalized by the amount of work of the engine. The oxides are made up of nitric oxide and nitrogen dioxide. One factor variable is the equivalence ratio, E, at which the engine was run. E is a measure of the richness of the air and fuel mixture; as E increases there is more fuel in the mixture. Another factor variable is C, the compression ratio to which the engine is set. C is the volume inside the cylinder when the piston is retracted, divided by the volume when the piston is at its maximum point of penetration into the cylinder.

As with coplots of scattered data, the given panel in Figure 3.68 is at
the top and the dependence panels are below. Consider the $(1,1)$
dependence panel. E has been set to a specific conditioning value, 0.535.
Then $g(C, 0.535)$ has been evaluated for equally spaced values of C
ranging from the minimum value of C in the data to the maximum. On
the panel, the values of g are graphed against the equally spaced values
of C. The same method is used on the other dependence panels, but for
different conditioning values of E. There are 16 equally spaced
conditioning values ranging from the minimum value of E in the data to
the maximum; the given panel shows the 16 values.

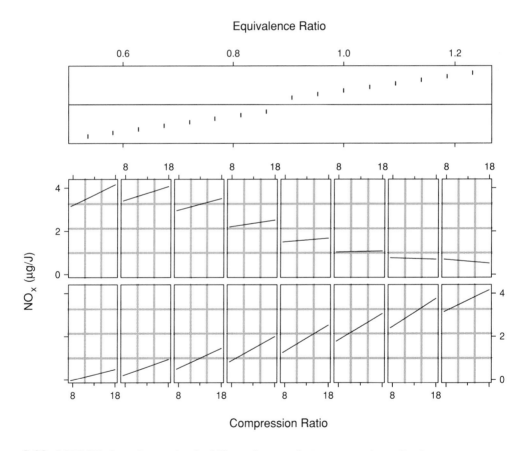

3.68 COPLOT. A coplot graphs the NO_x surface against compression ratio given
equivalence ratio. The curves are banked by an aspect ratio of 2 vcm/hcm. Banking to
$45°$ results in an aspect ratio that is too large.

Figure 3.68 shows that given E, g is linear in C. As the conditioning values of E increase from the lowest values, the slopes of the lines first increase until E is about 0.8, and then decrease to zero. Thus there is a strong interaction between C and E.

Figure 3.69 is a coplot of the NO_x surface against E for 16 conditioning values of C. Figure 3.69 shows that g varies in a highly nonlinear way as a function of E given C. The maximum of g increases by about 1 $\mu g/J$ as the conditioning values of C go from the minimum to the maximum; the value of E at which this maximum occurs is always close to 0.9.

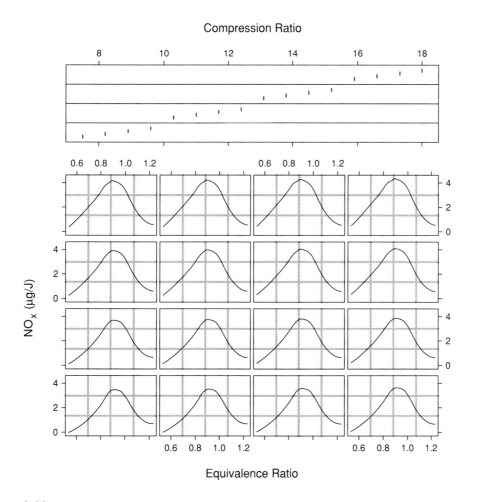

3.69 COPLOT. A coplot graphs the NO_x surface against equivalence ratio given compression ratio. The curves are banked to 45°.

3.12   Brushing

Data display on a computer screen allows the use of a powerful capability: *direct-manipulation methods.* The user visually addresses a display using an input device such as a mouse, and causes the display to change in real time. There are many ways to change the graphical image on the screen, and they are all graphical methods.

Brushing is one particularly useful direct-manipulation method [6]. Only a few of the uses will be described here; the reader should appreciate that it is no small challenge to describe a direct-manipulation computer graphical method, with dynamic elements that change in real time, on the static pages of a book.

One use of brushing is to carry out conditioning for scattered data to study how a response depends on one factor given the values of a second factor. This, of course, is the task carried out by the coplot, discussed in Section 3.10 (pp. 198–202); conditioning by brushing is a direct-manipulation counterpart of the coplot.

Brushing is illustrated in Figure 3.70. The data are the measurements from the rubber specimen experiment discussed in Section 3.10 (pp. 198–202). The principal direct-manipulation object in brushing is the *brush*: a rectangle on the screen, which is on the (1, 2) panel of Figure 3.70. The user can move the brush, and change its size and shape.

Figure 3.70 shows the result of brushing when the *highlight* operation has been selected. The data in this example consist of 30 points in a three-dimensional space. Each panel in the figure is a projection of the points onto a plane. When the brush encloses graphed values on one panel it selects a subset of the points in three dimensions; the data for these points are highlighted on all panels by filled circles. As the brush is moved, different points are selected, and the highlighting changes instantaneously. For example, in Figure 3.71 the brush has moved to the right on the (1, 2) panel.

Let us now consider what this highlighting has shown us about the rubber data. In Figure 3.70 the brush was positioned so that points with low values of hardness are highlighted. Look at the (2, 3) panel. The highlighted points are a graph of abrasion loss against tensile strength for low values of hardness; in other words, we see the dependence of abrasion loss on tensile strength with hardness held fixed, or nearly so. The highlighted points show that for hardness held to low values there is a nonlinear dependence of abrasion loss on tensile strength.

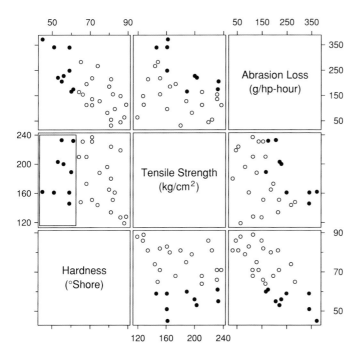

3.70 BRUSHING. The brush is the rectangle on the (1, 2) panel. The data for points selected by the brush are highlighted on all panels. When the brush is moved by the user, different points are selected and the highlighting changes instantaneously. In this figure points with low values of hardness are selected. The (2, 3) panel shows that for hardness held fixed to low values, abrasion loss depends nonlinearly on tensile strength.

This section presents two uses of color that genuinely transmit information from display to viewer. One is to render different categories of graphical elements in different colors to provide efficient assembly of the categories, that is, to allow us to see each category as a whole, mentally filtering out the other categories. In this application, color is encoding a categorical variable. The second use is encoding the values of a numerical function of two factor variables by a color level plot. In this application, color is encoding a quantitative variable.

Encoding a Categorical Variable

Color provides efficient visual assembly of different categories of graphical elements because our visual system does a marvelous job of assembling different objects with the same color. In particular it provides a powerful solution to the problem attacked in Section 3.5 (pp. 154–165) — enhancing visual assembly for superposed data sets.

In Figure 3.73, which appeared earlier in Section 3.5 (pp. 154–165), texture symbols encode a categorical variable — animal group. Figure I at the beginning of the book also graphs the data but with the animal group encoded by color. While texture symbols can provide an adequate encoding, color encoding often does better, allowing even more efficient visual assembly. The details of the color encoding are given in Section 4.3 (pp. 230–233).

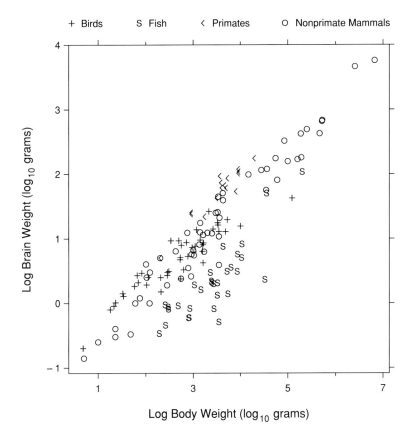

3.73 TEXTURE SYMBOLS. Log brain weights are graphed against log body weights for four categories of animals. Texture plotting symbols encode the animal categories.

Encoding a Quantitative Variable

One data type that arises frequently in science and technology is a function of two variables, $g(u, v)$, defined for values of u and v in the plane. Geometrically, the function is a surface in three dimensions. Two-variable functions arise from mathematical equations, from computer simulations, from fitting surfaces to noisy data, and from a variety of other sources.

One way to display a function of two variables is a color *level plot*. Figure II at the beginning of the book shows an example. The two variables are the coordinate locations in the desert of Western Australia; on the display they are labeled "northing" and "easting", a local coordinate system set up for convenience that has nothing to do with compass directions. The function value is the resistivity of the soil.

A *level* is an interval of values along the measurement scale of a function. The *level region* for the level is the set of (u, v) values in the plane whose function values lie in the level interval. A color level plot encodes different level regions by different colors. In Figure II there are 10 intervals, ranging from the minimum to the maximum function value.

There are two desiderata in choosing a color encoding of the quantitative values of a function. First, we typically want effortless perception of the order of the values. For example, effortless perception means we do not have to constantly refer to a key. Second, we want clearly perceived boundaries between adjacent levels. Achieving these two desiderata is difficult because they play against one another; it is easy to achieve one or the other, but hard to achieve both simultaneously. The color encoding in Figure II is a good compromise. There are two hues, cyan and magenta; as we move from the middle of the scale to the extremes, the color darkens. The details of the color encoding are given in Section 4.3 (pp. 230–233).

3.14   Statistical Variation

Measurements vary. Even when all controllable variables are kept constant, measurements vary because of uncontrollable variables or measurement error. One of the important functions of graphs in science and technology is to show the variation.

There are two very different domains of showing variation in data. One is to show the actual variation in the measurements, that is, to show the *empirical distribution* of the data. The second domain is the *sample-to-sample variation of a statistic*.

Empirical Distribution of the Data

When the goal is to convey just the empirical distribution of the data and not to make *formal* statistical inferences about a population distribution from which the data might have come, we can use the graphical methods for showing data distributions that were discussed in Section 3.3 (pp. 132–149). The box plots in Figure 3.74 are an example.

The data in Figure 3.74 are from an interesting experiment in bin packing [7]. There are k numbers, called weights, in the interval zero to u, where u is a positive number less than or equal to one. There are bins of size one, and the object is to pack the weights into those bins; no overflow is allowed, and we can use as many bins as necessary, but the goal is to use as few as possible. Unfortunately, to do this in an optimal manner is an NP-complete problem, which means that for anything but very small values of k, the computation time is enormous. Fortunately, there are heuristic algorithms which, while not optimal, do an extremely good job of packing. The heuristic algorithm tested in the experiment is called *first fit decreasing*. The weights are ordered from largest to smallest and are packed in that order. For each weight the first bin is tried; if it has room, the weight is inserted and if not, the second bin is

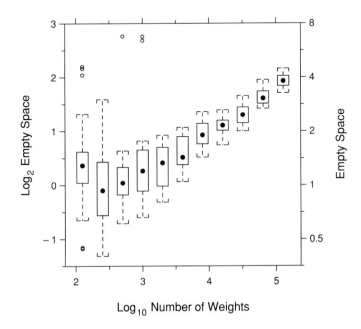

3.74 SHOWING EMPIRICAL VARIATION. For each value of log number of weights there are 25 measurements of log empty space whose distribution is summarized by a box plot.

tried; if the second bin has room, the weight is inserted and if not, the third bin is tried; the algorithm proceeds in this way until a bin with room, possibly a completely empty one, is found.

In the experiment, the weights were randomly selected from the interval 0 to 0.8. The number of weights, k, for each simulation run took one of 11 values: 125, 250, 500, and so forth by factors of 2 up to 128,000. There were 25 runs for each of the 11 different numbers of weights. For each run of the experiment, the performance of the algorithm was measured by the total amount of empty space in the bins that were used. Figure 3.74 shows box plots of the logs of the 25 empty space values for each value of the log of k.

Another method for showing the variation in the data, one that is very common in science and technology, is to use a plotting symbol and error bars to portray the *sample mean* and the *sample standard deviation*. Suppose the values of the data are $x_1, \ldots, x_n$ then the sample mean is

$$\bar{x} = \frac{1}{n} \sum_{i=1}^{n} x_i$$

and the sample standard deviation is

$$s = \sqrt{\frac{1}{n-1} \sum_{i=1}^{n} (x_i - \bar{x})^2} \,.$$

Figure 3.75 uses a filled circle and error bars to show the mean plus and minus one sample standard deviation for each of the 11 data sets of the bin packing example. This graph does a poor job of conveying the variation in the data. For example, it camouflages the outliers: the unusually high values of empty space that occur for low numbers of weights. The box plots in Figure 3.74 do a far better job of conveying the empirical variation of the data.

This result — the mean and sample standard deviation doing a poor job of conveying the distribution of the data — is frequently the case, because without any other information about the data, these two summary statistics tell us little about where the data lie. This is further illustrated in Figure 3.76. The top panel shows four sets of made-up data. The four sets have the same sample size, the same sample mean, and the same sample standard deviation, but the behavior of the four empirical distributions is radically different. The means and sample standard deviations in the bottom panel do not capture the variation of the four data sets.

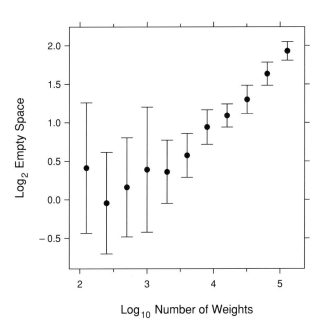

3.75 MEANS AND SAMPLE STANDARD DEVIATIONS. Showing just means and sample standard deviations is often a poor way to convey the variation in the data. This example shows means and sample standard deviations for the 11 sets of data graphed in Figure 3.74. The outliers in the data are not conveyed.

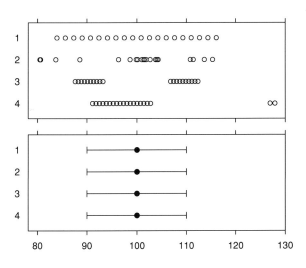

3.76 MEANS AND SAMPLE STANDARD DEVIATIONS. Means and sample standard deviations cannot characterize the wide variety of distributions that data can have. Four sets of data are graphed in the top panel and their means and sample standard deviations are graphed in the bottom panel. The four distributions have the same numbers of observations, the same means, and the same sample standard deviations, but the distributions are very different.

There is an exception to this poor performance of the sample standard deviation. If the empirical distribution of the data is well approximated by a normal probability distribution then we know approximately what percentage of the data lies between the mean plus and minus a constant times s. For example, approximately 68% lies between $\bar{x} \pm s$, approximately 50% lies between $\bar{x} \pm 0.67s$, and approximately 95% lies between $\bar{x} \pm 1.96s$. However, empirical distributions are often not well approximated by the normal. The normal distribution is symmetric, but real data are often skewed to the right. The normal distribution does not have wild observations, but real data often do.

One approach to showing the empirical variation in the data might be to check how well the empirical distribution is approximated by a normal, and then use the mean and sample standard deviation to summarize the distribution if the approximation is a good one. For example, one method for checking normality is a normal probability plot [26]. If the goal were to make inferences about the population distribution then checking normality is a vital matter and well worth the effort, as will be discussed shortly. But going through the trouble of checking normality, when the *only* goal is to show the empirical variation in the data, is often needless effort. The direct, easy, and rapid approach to showing the empirical variation in the data is to show the data. This means using graphical methods such as box plots and quantile plots to show the empirical distribution of the data. Thus, after this long discussion we have been led to the following circular advice: if the goal is to show the data, then show the data.

Sample-to-Sample Variation of a Statistic

Let us consider a simple but common sampling situation. Suppose we have a random sample of measurements, x_i for $i = 1$ to n, from a population distribution. Suppose we are interested in making inferences about the mean, μ, of the population distribution. The population mean can be estimated by the sample mean, $\bar{x}$, of the data.

The sample mean is a *statistic*, a numerical value based on the sample, and if we took a new sample of size n, $\bar{x}$ would be different; the variation of $\bar{x}$ from one sample of size n to the next is the sample-to-sample variation of $\bar{x}$.

$\overline{x}$ also has a population distribution and the sample-to-sample variation of $\overline{x}$ is characterized by it. Suppose σ is the standard deviation of the population distribution of the data, then the standard deviation of the population distribution of $\overline{x}$ is $\sigma/\sqrt{n}$. As n gets large this standard deviation gets small, the population distribution of $\overline{x}$ closes in on μ, and $\overline{x}$ varies less and less from sample to sample. The standard deviation of the mean, like μ, is unknown but it can be estimated; since s, the sample standard deviation, is an estimate of σ, $\sigma/\sqrt{n}$ can be estimated by $s/\sqrt{n}$, which is often called the *standard error of the mean*, although *estimated standard deviation of the sample mean* is the full name.

One-Standard-Error Bars

The current convention in science and technology for portraying sample-to-sample variation of a statistic is to graph error bars to portray plus and minus one standard error of the statistic, just the way the sample standard deviation is used to summarize the empirical variation of the data.

Figure 3.77 shows statistics from experiments on graphical perception [36]. Subjects in the three experiments judged quantitative information for seven methods of encoding the information. The methods for each experiment are described by the labels in Figure 3.77. For each encoding method in each experiment a statistic was computed that measures the absolute error; the statistic is averaged across all subjects and across all judgments for that method. The filled circles in Figure 3.77 graph the statistics. The subjects in each experiment are thought of as a random sample from the population of subjects who can understand graphs. If we took new samples of subjects, the statistics shown in Figure 3.77 would vary. The error bars in Figure 3.77 show plus and minus one standard error of the statistics. (The statistics in this example are not means; the standard errors are computed from a formula that is more complicated than that for the standard error of the mean, however, we do not need to be concerned with the formula here.)

Now the critical point is the following. A standard error of a statistic has value only insofar as it conveys information about *confidence intervals*. The standard error by itself conveys little. It is confidence intervals that convey the sample-to-sample variation of a statistic.

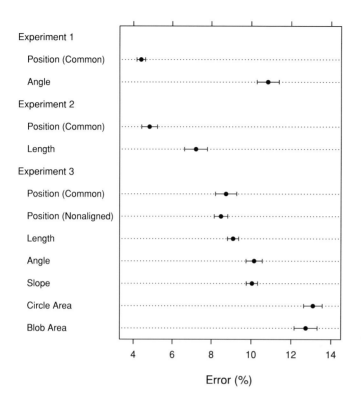

3.77 ONE-STANDARD-ERROR BARS TO SHOW SAMPLE-TO-SAMPLE VARIATION. The filled circles show statistics from experiments on graphical perception. Each error bar, conforming to the convention in science and technology, shows plus and minus one standard error. The interval formed by the error bars is a 68% confidence interval, which is not a particularly interesting interval. One standard error bars are a naive translation of the convention for numerical reporting of sample-to-sample variation.

In some cases confidence intervals are formed by taking plus and minus a multiple of the standard error. For example, suppose the x_i are a sample from a normal population distribution, suppose the statistic is $\overline{x}$, and suppose our purpose is to estimate the mean, μ, of the population distribution. Let $t_d(\alpha)$ be a number such that the probability between $-t_d(\alpha)$ and $t_d(\alpha)$ for a t-distribution with d degrees of freedom is α. Then the interval

$$\overline{x} - t_{n-1}(\alpha)s/\sqrt{n} \quad \text{to} \quad \overline{x} + t_{n-1}(\alpha)s/\sqrt{n}$$

is a $100\alpha\%$ confidence interval for the mean. In other words, μ is in the above interval for $100\alpha\%$ of the samples of size n drawn from the population distribution. This confidence interval is just the sample mean plus and minus a constant times the standard error of the mean. If n is about 60 or above, the t-distribution is very nearly a normal distribution. This means

$$t_{n-1}(0.5) \approx 0.67 \qquad t_{n-1}(0.68) \approx 1 \qquad t_{n-1}(0.95) \approx 1.96 \; .$$

Thus, in this situation, $\overline{x} \pm s/\sqrt{n}$ is approximately a 68% confidence interval, $\overline{x} \pm 0.67s/\sqrt{n}$ is approximately a 50% interval, and $\overline{x} \pm 1.96s/\sqrt{n}$ is approximately a 95% interval.

There are other sampling situations, however, where confidence intervals are *not* based on standard errors. For example, if the x_i are from an exponential distribution, then confidence intervals for the population mean are based on the sample mean, but they do not involve the standard error of the mean [81].

How did it happen that the solidly entrenched convention in science and technology is to show one standard error on graphs? In some cases plus and minus one standard error has no useful, easy interpretation. True, in many cases plus and minus one standard error is a 68% confidence interval; Figure 3.77 is one example. Is a 68% confidence interval interesting? Are confidence intervals thought about at all when error bars are put on graphs?

It is likely that the one-standard-error bar of graphical communication in science and technology is a result of the convention for numerical communication. If we want to communicate sample-to-sample variation numerically in cases where confidence intervals are based on standard errors, then it is reasonable to communicate the standard error and let the reader do some arithmetic, either mentally or otherwise, to get confidence intervals. A reasonable conjecture is that this numerical convention was simply brought to graphs. But the difficulty with this translation is that we are visually locked into what is shown by the error bars; it is hard to multiply the bars visually by some constant to get a desired visual confidence interval on the graph. Another difficulty, of course, is that confidence intervals are not always based on standard errors.

Two-Tiered Error Bars

Figure 3.78 uses *two-tiered error bars* to convey the sample-to-sample variation of the statistics from the perception experiment. For each statistic the ends of the inner error bars, which are marked by the short vertical lines, are a 50% confidence interval; the ends of the outer error bars are a 95% confidence interval. When confidence intervals are quoted numerically in scientific writings the level is almost always a

The model is presented in Section 4.1 (pp. 223–227). In subsequent sections, the model serves as a framework for studies of display methods. The studies accomplish two goals. They provide the justification for a number of display methods introduced in earlier chapters, and they provide guidance for carrying out other studies.

Section 4.2 (pp. 227–230) studies the display of two or more curves in the same scale-line rectangle. Superposed curves are simple to draw and ubiquitous, so it might be thought that there are no issues, but superposed curves create a major decoding problem.

Section 4.3 (pp. 230–233) is about color encoding: selecting the hues, saturations, and lightnesses of colors that encode data. There are two cases: color encoding a categorical variable, and color encoding a quantitative variable.

Section 4.4 (pp. 234–239) presents the rigorous study that led to texture symbols for encoding different groups of points on scatterplots.

Section 4.5 (pp. 240–243) studies visual reference grids for enhancing the comparison of data on juxtaposed panels. One of the basic laws of psychophysics, Weber's Law, is at the core of this issue.

Section 4.6 (pp. 244–250) studies methods for ordering categories on dot plots and multiway dot plots. These ordering methods can substantially enhance our visual decoding.

Section 4.7 (pp. 251–256) reviews the theory, the mathematics, and the experimentation that led to the discovery of banking to 45°.

Section 4.8 (pp. 256–258) presents an interesting aspect of scatterplots that affects our perception of the correlation between two variables.

Section 4.9 (pp. 259–261) studies encoding by position along a common scale, a display method that leads to efficient visual decoding.

Section 4.10 (pp. 262–269) is about pop charts: visual displays used largely in the mass media and in certain business presentations where the transmission of information is less of an issue, and glitzy display that does not tax the intellect is paramount. The section shows why three pop charts — pie charts, divided bar charts, and area charts — do not result in efficient visual decoding compared with other display methods.

4.1   The Model

Quantitative and Categorical Information

The information inside the data rectangle of a graph can be partitioned into *quantitative values* and *categorical values*. This is illustrated in the multiway dot plot in Figure 4.1. The data are from an agricultural experiment [63]. The response is barley yield and the factors are the growing site (6 categories), the barley variety (10 categories), and the year (2 categories). The yield variable is quantitative; it takes on numerical values. The site, variety, and year variables are categorical; their values are categories. For example, the site variable takes on one of six categorical values — "Waseca", "Crookston", "University Farm", and so forth. A year variable in many applications is quantitative, but in this application it is categorical in that it simply indicates two different growing seasons.

Scale Information and Physical Information

Categorical information and quantitative information each can be described in two ways: *scale* and *physical*. For a quantitative value, scale information is the value in the units of the data. For a categorical value, it is the name of the category. For the observation with the largest yield in Figure 4.1, the scale information is the following: (1) yield = 65 bushels/acre; (2) site = "Waseca"; (3) variety = "No. 462"; (4) year = "1931". The physical information on a graph is a description of the quantitative and categorical information after the removal of the tick labels and the names of categories. We retain the geometry of graphical elements and a breakup of the data into different subsets according to the categories. For the observation with the largest yield, the physical information is the following: (1) yield = 3.9 cm (along the horizontal scale); (2) site = "top panel"; (3) variety = "panel-level two from the bottom"; (4) year = "+".

Pattern Perception and Table Look-Up

The visual decoding of scale information is *table look-up*. For example, we use operations of table look-up to decode the scale

Estimation is the visual assessment of the relative magnitudes of two or more quantitative physical values, a and b. There are three progressive levels of this operation: *discrimination*, *ranking*, and *ratioing*. Discrimination is a judgment of whether $a = b$ or $a \neq b$. Ranking is a judgment of whether $a > b$, $a < b$, or $a = b$. Ratioing is a judgment of the value of a/b. As we move from discrimination to ranking to ratioing there is an increase in the amount of information derived from the judgment. In Figure 4.1, we estimate the lengths of the horizontal line segments connecting the "○" symbols to the "+" symbols to visually decode the magnitudes of the 1931 and 1932 yield differences. This is an estimation operation.

Three Operations of Table Look-Up

The three operations of table look-up in the model are *scanning*, *interpolation*, and *matching*. As with pattern perception, the efficiency is determined by speed and accuracy.

Consider the largest yield in Figure 4.1. To look up the scale value of yield we scan and interpolate: (1) scan perpendicularly up or down to fix a point along a horizontal scale line; (2) interpolate by estimating the distance from the point to the tick mark to the left or to the right as a fraction of the distance between tick marks. Then another process takes over; we read the tick mark labels and use the physical interpolation to convert to an interpolation in data units. For most people, the decoded scale value would be about 65 bushels/acre. To look up the scale value for variety we scan to the left to get "No. 462". To look up the scale value for site, we scan to the top of the panel to get "Waseca". To look up the scale value for year, we scan to the key and match the "+" encoding the value with the "+" in the key.

Using the Model to Study Display Methods

The model provides a collection of visual operations that are to be considered in the study of a display method. It does not prescribe which of its visual operations are important in any particular case, nor does it provide information about the efficiency of the important visual operations once they have been determined. Determinations of importance and efficiency must come from basic reasoning, the theory of visual perception, simple demonstration, and measured-response experiments. But the model does play a vital role in specifying a collection of operations that are central to graphical perception. Studying these operations can yield important information for judging the performance of display methods. The examples in the next sections demonstrate this.

4.2   Superposed Curves

Figure 4.2, also shown in Section 1.3 (pp. 16–21), graphs data published by William Playfair in 1786 [108]. The top panel displays the values of imports and exports between England and the East Indies. To visually decode the import data we judge the import curve. Each point along the curve encodes imports at a specific point in time. The detection and assembly of the points is exceedingly efficient, and the result is a gestalt, a visual whole that appears as a single object on the graph. The same statements hold for the export curve.

Also encoded by this graph are the amounts by which imports exceed exports. These quantities are encoded by vertical line segments that connect the two curves. Thus to visually decode differences between the curves we must detect the segments, assemble them, and then estimate their lengths. In this section we study the visual operations of pattern perception and table look-up for our decoding of the differences of curves.

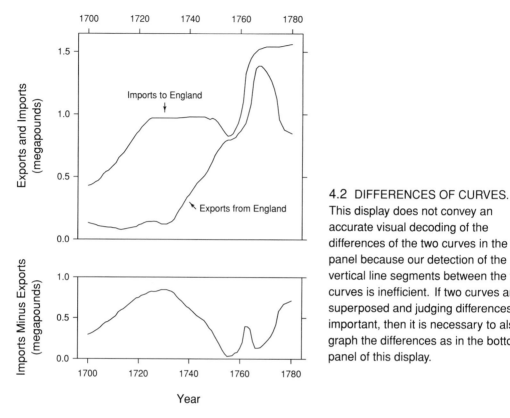

4.2 DIFFERENCES OF CURVES. This display does not convey an accurate visual decoding of the differences of the two curves in the top panel because our detection of the vertical line segments between the two curves is inefficient. If two curves are superposed and judging differences is important, then it is necessary to also graph the differences as in the bottom panel of this display.

Pattern Perception

Surprisingly, pattern perception for differences of curves can be exceedingly inaccurate. It is surprising because the superposing of two or more curves is such a ubiquitous graphical method and because the formation of the individual curve gestalts is so efficient. But simple demonstration shows clearly the inaccuracy.

Figure 4.2 provides a simple demonstration. During the period just after 1760 when both curves are rapidly increasing, the visual impression is that imports minus exports is not large and does not change by much. This is not the case. In the bottom panel of Figure 4.2, imports minus exports are graphed directly. Now, the differences form a curve, and the result is a far more accurate decoding of the information about imports minus exports. The behavior just after 1760 is quite different from how it appears in the top panel; there is a rapid rise to a peak and then a decrease.

Figure 4.3 provides another demonstration with made-up data. The visual impression is that the differences decrease from left to right, but the differences are constant.

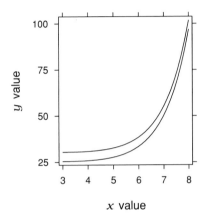

4.3 DIFFERENCES OF CURVES. The differences of the curves appear to decrease from left to right but they are constant.

The problem in judging the difference of two curves is not inaccurate estimation, but rather inaccurate detection. When the slopes of two superposed curves are steep, it is exceedingly difficult for our visual system to focus on the vertical distances between the curves. Our visual system detects minimum distances. For example in Figure 4.3 the minimum distances lie along perpendiculars to the tangents of the curves. As the slope increases, the distance along the perpendicular decreases, so the curves look closer as the slope increases. Our visual system does an accurate job of detecting, assembling and estimating the minimum distance segments; the problem is that they are the wrong segments and we cannot force our visual system to process the right segments without using slow sequential search.

Table Look-Up

Figure 4.2 also shows that table look-up for differences of superposed curves is much less efficient than for a direct graphing of the differences. Consider the decoding of the scale value of the difference for 1740. In the bottom panel a single horizontal scan to a vertical scale line together with an interpolation result in a value of about 0.7 megapounds. In the top panel of Figure 4.2 we must either perform two such scans and interpolations or match the vertical distance between the curves at 1740 with a vertical distance along a vertical scale line.

Remedies

Playfair graphed the import-export data using the method of the top panel of Figure 4.2, yet much of his discussion focused on the balance of payments, the differences of the curves, so his display method was not adequate to the task.

One display method for curves is to superpose them on one panel and graph differences on another. This is an attractive method if there are just two curves; Figure 4.2 is one example. The remedy provides both improved pattern perception and improved table look-up.

Another remedy is to juxtapose curves on separate panels. While pattern perception of differences is not as efficient as a direct graphing of differences, and table look-up is not enhanced, the juxtaposition does eliminate the distortion of pattern perception caused by superposition. This remedy is attractive when there are many curves as, for example, on the conditioning plots of functions in Section 3.11 (pp. 203–205). And when this juxtaposition is used, visual reference grids can enhance our pattern perception; the reason for this is given in Section 4.5 (pp. 240–243).

4.3   Color Encoding

There are two uses of color that genuinely enhance the visual decoding of information from graphs. One is encoding different categories of graphical elements in different colors. Figure I at the beginning of the book is one example. Another use is the color level plot: a display of a function of two variables, $z = g(x, y)$, where x and y are encoded by position in the plane and z is encoded by color at the position. Figure II at the beginning of the book is an example. These two uses of color were discussed in Section 3.13 (pp. 209–212). Here, we discuss in detail the color encodings.

The two uses of color are distinct and require different methods. Coloring different groups of graphical elements is an encoding of a categorical variable. For example, in Figure I the categorical variable is the animal group. The goal is an encoding that makes the visual operation of assembly as efficient as possible. For a color level plot a quantitative variable is encoded. For example, in Figure II the encoded variable is soil resistivity. The goal is an encoding that makes the visual operation of estimation as efficient as possible.

Color Specification by HSL

The processing of light by our visual system is an amazing feat. Light with a single color is a mixture of energies at different wavelengths in the visible spectrum ranging from about 380 nanometers to 770 nanometers. The variation in the amounts of radiation at the different wavelengths accounts for our different color perceptions.

The physical characterization of the light requires the specification of the amounts of radiation at all wavelengths in the visible spectrum. But our perception of color can be described accurately by just three numbers that are derivable from the radiation amounts [50,119]. If two different light sources with different mixtures of wavelengths have the same three numbers, we judge their colors to be the same.

One three-value system is the HSL system: hue, saturation and lightness [50,119]. Hue is what we typically mean in everyday language when we refer to color; hue is described by terms such as green, blue, yellow, magenta, and so forth. Hue is measured in degrees from 0° to 360° since there is a circularity to our perception of hue. (0° and 360° describe the same hue.) The following are the hues of six colors that are equally spaced around the color circle: red = 0°, yellow = 60°, green = 120°, cyan = 180°, blue = 240°, magenta = 300°. In Figure I there are four hues: cyan, magenta, orange (30°), and green. In Figure II there are two hues: cyan and magenta. Lightness refers to how light or dark a color appears. Saturation refers to how pale or deep a color appears. For example, a deep red is highly saturated but a pink is desaturated. If the hue and lightness of a color are kept constant, and the saturation is decreased, the color becomes paler until, when the saturation is zero, the color becomes a gray. For the magentas in Figure II the saturation increases and the lightness decreases as resistivity decreases from the middle of the scale to the smallest values. For the cyans, the saturation increases and the lightness decreases as resistivity increases from the middle of the scale to the largest values.

Assembly and Ranking

There are three properties of color perception that provide principles for the two color encoding tasks: encoding a categorical variable and encoding a quantitative variable.

First, changing hue can provide efficient discrimination of colors. This is strongly supported by both theory and experiment [83,120]. Thus we can use changing hue to provide efficient visual assembly when we encode a categorical variable. In Figure I, assembly of the different groups of points is efficient because the different hues are discriminable. Shortly, we will specify five colors that provide good assembly; four of them are used in Figure II.

Second, if hue is held fixed we can perceive an ordering as either lightness changes or saturation changes. Thus we can use changing lightness and saturation to provide efficient ranking when we encode a quantitative variable. Consider the magentas in Figure II. As resistivity increases from the smallest values to the middle values, the increase in lightness and the decrease in saturation act in concert to provide a strong sense of order. A similar statement holds for the cyans. Shortly, we will give a precise specification of the colors used in Figure II.

Third, we cannot effortlessly perceive an ordering to changing hue. Thus an encoding of a quantitative variable that incorporates changes through many hues does not result in efficient ranking. As Travis [119] puts it, "It is erroneous to assume that we have some hard-wired intuitions for a spectral sequence (i.e. red, orange, yellow, green, blue, indigo, violet)." And as Tufte puts it [122], "the mind's eye does not readily give an order to ROYGBIV." In Figure II, there are two hues, which might seem to ignore this principle of hue perception. But two hues are used to achieve another perceptual goal: clearly perceived boundaries between adjacent levels of the color encoding. Two hues provide somewhat more color variation than just one. True, we do now need to remember that values encoded by cyan are greater than those encoded by magenta, but this does not unduly burden the ranking operation.

CMYK Specification of Colors for Color Encoding

Another method for specifying color is the CMYK system: cyan, magenta, yellow, and black [50,99]. This is the standard system used by printers to produce color on paper. First, each of the four basis colors can be mixed with white; a 75%–cyan is 75% cyan and 25% white. Colors are described by combinations of mixed basis colors. For example, in Figure I the orange mixes a 50%–magenta and a 100%–yellow in equal amounts. We will use the CMYK system to specify a set of colors for encoding a categorical variable and another set for encoding a quantitative variable; we use CMYK because it leads to a simple description. But there are transformations that can translate CMYK to HSL values or to RGB, the red, green, and blue system used for computer screens [50,99].

Five colors that provide good visual assembly of the categories of a categorical variable are 100%–cyan, 100%–magenta, 100%–yellow mixed equally with 100%–cyan (green), 50%–magenta mixed equally with 100%–yellow (orange), and 100%–cyan mixed equally with 50%–magenta (light blue). The first four of these are used in Figure I. Actually, a better statement is that the first four are attempted in Figure I since the achieved colors of hardcopy output inevitably vary somewhat from what is specified.

The color encoding in Figure II provides efficient ranking of a quantitative variable. From the middle to the extremes, the cyan ranges from 20%–cyan to 100%–cyan in steps of 20%–cyan, and the magenta ranges from 20%–magenta to 100%–magenta in steps of 20%–magenta. This method provides efficient ranking because it allows accurate ordering and it allows a sufficient number of distinct colors. But there is a bound on the number of colors that can be used if the distinction is to be maintained. Because of the delicacy of color reproduction, only 10 have been used in Figure II. At a computer screen it is possible to drive the number up to 15 or so, but using a significantly greater number typically results in a perceptual merging of some of the adjacent colors. Actually, more than 10 colors are used in Figure II, but the additional ones occur just at boundaries of level regions and are only barely perceptible. This *anti-aliasing* uses standard methods to give the boundaries a smooth look [26].

4.4   *Texture Symbols*

Figure 4.4 graphs brain weights against body weights for four groups of animals. The animal group, a categorical variable, is encoded by different symbol types. The selection of the plotting symbols for such an encoding on a scatterplot substantially affects our ability to detect and assemble each group of points.

If color is available, the color encoding method for categorical variables given in Section 4.3 (pp. 230–233) provides highly efficient detection and assembly that typically performs better than different symbol types in black and white. But the assumption in this section is that color is not available.

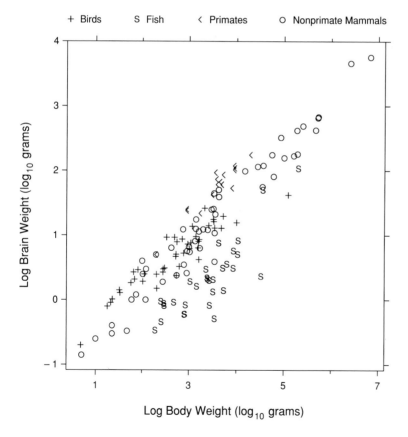

4.4 TEXTURE SYMBOLS. Animal group, which is a categorical variable, is encoded by texture symbols, which provide efficient detection and assembly of the four groups of points.

The symbols in Figure 4.4 are from the texture symbol set introduced in Section 3.5 (pp. 154–165). Compared with many other symbol sets, the texture set provides highly efficient detection and assembly. In Figure 4.5 another encoding set is used — the first letters of the group names — and the assembly is poor. In this section we will present the scientific investigations that led to the choice of the texture symbols.

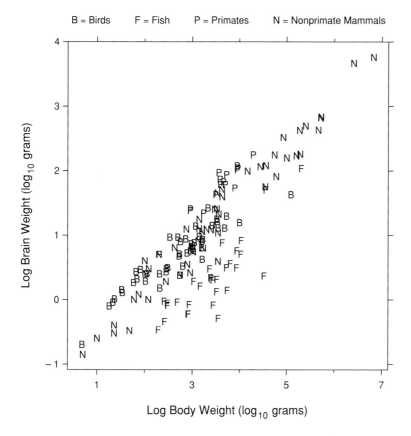

4.5 LETTERS. The plotting symbols are the first letters of the group names. Detection and assembly are less efficient than for the texture symbols.

Detection

Suppose that symbols overlap as in Figure 4.4. To enhance detection we will choose from symbols that are made up of curves and line segments. Such symbols enhance the visual operation of detection when the symbols overlap. Filled symbols such as filled circles tend to form uninterpretable blobs in the presence of overlap, so detection is degraded.

Assembly

Imagine a room with a plaid rug and a polka-dot wall. The wall and the rug have distinct *textures*: micropatterns with much local variation that nevertheless take on a uniform appearance to our visual system [69]. Where the wall and rug meet, the visual system perceives a clearly defined boundary between the texture patterns. But different micropatterns with very different local features can appear much like one another or even the same.

Each panel of Figure 4.6 has two micropatterns, left and right, with different local features. There is substantial variation in the perceptual salience of the boundaries between the patterns. There is a strong boundary for "+" and "○", a weaker one for "T" and "L", and none for "R" and "mirror-R".

What properties of the local features of micropatterns result in strong boundaries and what properties are ignored? This question has been intensively studied by vision researchers because texture perception is one of the important processes of our visual algorithms [69,78,88,90,120]. Fortunately for our search for plotting symbols on graphs with overlap, many of these studies investigated micropatterns formed by symbols consisting of lines and curves, exactly the domain of symbols that are candidates for graphs. Two symbols that provide strong boundaries on micropatterns such as those in Figure 4.6, also provide efficient assembly on scatterplots, so we can use these studies in texture perception to select a symbol set.

Kröse [77,78] ran experiments in which subjects determined the presence or absence of a single occurrence of a symbol of a certain type drawn among a texture pattern of symbols of another type. They saw each picture for 80 milliseconds. The percentage of correct answers, corrected for guessing, measures the degree of texture discrimination. The second column of Table 4.1 shows percentages from the Kröse experiments for seven of the symbol pairs in Figure 4.6.

A second method of study of texture perception is the image processing of texture patterns using algorithms of computational vision that attempt to reproduce the algorithms of the human visual system [90]. Malik and Perona used methods of computational vision to study the 10 pairs of micropatterns in Figure 4.6 [88]. They applied a texture algorithm to each pair to produce a texture image. To determine the degree of texture discriminability, they computed a measure from each image of how distinct the vertical boundary is between the two regions of symbols. This measure is shown in the third column of Table 4.1 for the 10 symbol pairs. The order from smallest to largest of the algorithmic measure is nearly the same as that for the experimental.

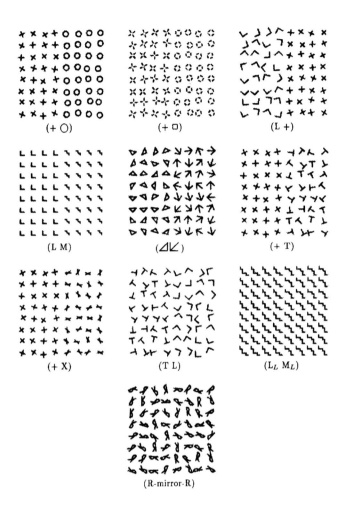

4.6 TEXTURES. Each panel shows two micropatterns formed by symbols. The perceptual salience of the boundaries between the pairs varies substantially. Studies of texture perception provide information for selecting plotting symbols for graphs.

Table 4.1 TEXTURE DISCRIMINATION.

Texture Pair	Experiment	Algorithm
$+\ \circ$	100	407
$+\ \square$	88.1	225
$L\ +$	68.6	203
$L\ M$		165
$\Delta\ \downarrow$	52.3	159
$+\ T$	37.6	120
$+\ X$	30.3	104
$T\ L$	30.6	90
$L_L\ M_L$		85
R mirror-R		50

The information from Table 4.1 together with a number of simple demonstrations were the basis for the choice of the five texture symbols given in Section 3.5 (pp. 154–165). The symbols, which have an order, are "$\circ$", "$+$", "$<$", "s", and "w". If there are two groups, the first two symbols are used. If there are three groups, the first three are used, and so forth. Clearly, Table 4.1 gives strong support for using "$\circ$" and "$+$" for two or more groups; this pair has the highest level of discrimination of the 10 pairs. The symbol "$<$" is third since it does well against "$+$" in Table 4.1, and simple demonstration suggests that it does well against "$\circ$". The fourth symbol, "s", was picked solely on the basis of simple demonstration. The fifth symbol, "w", is an approximation of the symbol labeled "M" in Figure 4.6.

4.5   Visual Reference Grids

Visual reference grids were discussed in Section 3.6 (pp. 166–167) and have been used throughout the book to enhance the visual decoding of displays with juxtaposed panels.

Table Look-Up vs. Pattern Perception

Grids on graphs are, of course, an old idea. Originally, they were drawn to enhance table look-up. This was important because graphs were in part archival: they recorded data for detailed recovery of their values later. Also, grids appeared because they were used as an aid to graph production, which was done by hand. Because of their two purposes, table look-up grids were drawn at simple numbers, the simple numbers used for tick marks today. Because the purpose of visual reference grids is to enhance pattern perception and not table look-up, it is not important that the grid lines be drawn at simple numbers; it is only vital that the same grid be drawn on all panels.

Table look-up grids have largely been abandoned in the display of scientific data because of the ubiquitous use of computers to produce graphs and communicate data. But visual reference grids remain as an important display method.

Weber's Law

Our study of visual reference grids will make use of *Weber's Law*, formulated by the 19th century psychophysicist E. H. Weber [4]. It is one of the fundamental laws of human perception. Suppose x is the magnitude of a physical attribute; to be specific let it be the length of a line segment. Let $w_p(x)$ be a positive number such that a line of length $x + w_p(x)$ is discriminated with probability p to be longer than the line of length x. Weber's Law states that for fixed p,

$$w_p(x) = k_p x \, ,$$

where k_p does not depend on x. The law appears to describe reality extremely well for many perceptual judgments including length, area, and volume.

One implication of Weber's Law is that we need a fixed percentage increase in line length to achieve detection. For example, it is easy to detect a difference between two lines of length 2 cm and 2.5 cm, because the percentage increase of the second over the first is 25%; however, it is much harder to detect a difference between two lines that are 50 cm and 50.5 cm, even though the difference is also 0.5 cm, because the percentage increase is only 1%.

In the left panel of Figure 4.7 there are two solid rectangles with unequal vertical lengths. It is difficult to determine which length is greater. In the right panel, the two solid rectangles are embedded in two frames that have equal vertical lengths. Now we can accurately discriminate the vertical lengths of the solid bars; the right length is greater.

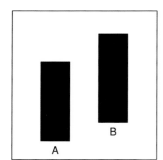 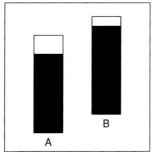

4.7 WEBER'S LAW. The solid rectangles in the left panel have unequal vertical lengths that are difficult to discriminate. In the right panel the solid rectangles are embedded in frames that have equal vertical lengths and now we can accurately discriminate the lengths. Weber's Law explains why.

Weber's Law explains our differing accuracies of length estimation in Figure 4.7. In the left panel our estimation is not accurate enough to discriminate the length differences because the percentage difference is small. In the right panel the two rectangles formed by the empty spaces at the tops of the frames have vertical lengths whose absolute differences — that is, differences in cm — are the same as those of the solid bars, but whose percentage differences are much greater. Because of Weber's law, we can readily perceive that the vertical length of the left empty rectangle is greater. The vertical lengths of the two frames, which have been drawn to be equal, do indeed appear equal to us. The visual system combines this conclusion of equality of the frames with the conclusion that the vertical length of the left empty rectangle is greater to infer that the vertical length of the right solid rectangle is greater.

Pattern Perception

In Figure 4.8 eight curves are graphed twice in juxtaposed panels, once in the two columns of panels to the left and once in the two columns to the right.

The operations of detection, assembly, and estimation for decoding information about each curve in Figure 4.8 are exceedingly efficient. The result is a gestalt, a curve object that we see as a single perceptual unit. But the comparison of curves on different panels is an entirely different visual process. Consider the decoding of the minima of the eight curves in the left two columns. There are different ways this can be done. One is to detect and assemble the vertical line segments that extend from the bottom lines of the boxes to the points on the curves where the minima occur, and then carry out estimation of the lengths. The detection and assembly must be carried out by a highly attentive sequential search process with shifts of our eyes from one panel to the next. No gestalt forms as it does for the visual decoding of a single curve because the visual operations are much slower. We cannot readily hold all segments in short term memory, and even our cognitive processing, our conscious conclusion about relative values, must be built up from a sequence of comparisons of subsets of values. Nevertheless, the comparison of minima and other commensurate aspects of curves on separate panels is an informative visual process.

The Application of Weber's Law

Weber's Law explains why visual reference grids enhance pattern perception. The grids allow us to convert estimation of lengths with small percentage differences to estimation with much larger percentage differences which, by Weber's Law, means an increase in accuracy. Figure 4.8 illustrates this. Consider the values of the minima of the five curves with deep troughs. As we just saw, in the left two columns we can compare the minima by judgment of the lengths of the vertical line segments that extend from the bottom lines of the boxes to the points on the curves where the minima occur. But in the right two columns we can compare the minima by estimation of the five line segments extending from the minima to the horizontal grid lines just above them, or by

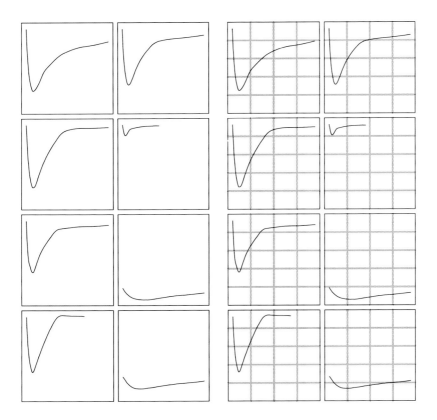

4.8 VISUAL REFERENCE GRIDS. Eight curves are graphed twice, once in the two columns of panels to the left and once to the right. The right columns have visual reference grids that enhance pattern perception; they enable more efficient comparisons of patterns on different panels. The increased efficiency is explained by Weber's Law.

estimation of the five line segments extending down to the grid lines just below. Each of these two collections of five segments has lengths whose pairwise percentage differences are greater than those of the segments to the bottom lines of the boxes.

One response to this discussion might be that we should superpose as many data sets as possible to reduce the comparison of patterns on different panels. For certain types of graphs — for example, for scatterplots — this can make sense. But as we saw in Section 4.2 (pp. 227–230), superposed curves introduce serious biases in our judgments of differences of curves because of faulty detection.

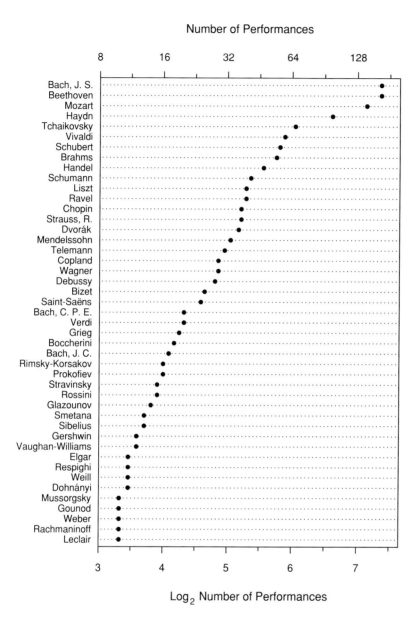

Number of Performances

Log₂ Number of Performances

4.9 ORDER FOR DOT PLOTS. The data on this dot plot are ordered from smallest to largest. This enhances our visual decoding of the distribution of the values along the measurement scale.

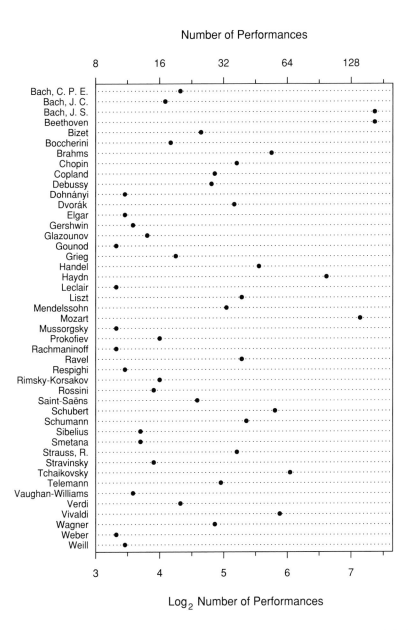

Number of Performances

4.10 ORDER FOR DOT PLOTS. The data on this dot plot are ordered alphabetically. This degrades our visual decoding of the distribution of the values along the measurement scale.

Order is important for multiway dot plots as well. Figure 4.11 graphs the logarithms of livestock counts from a census of farm animals in 26 countries [14]. The livestock variable is encoded by the panels and the country variable is encoded by the levels of each panel. The countries are assigned to the levels so that the country medians increase from bottom to top. The median of the five observations for Albania is the smallest country median. Norway has the next smallest country median, and Russia *et al.* has the largest. The panels are ordered so that the livestock medians increase from left to right and from bottom to top. The median for horses is the smallest, and the median for poultry is the largest.

The category orderings in Figure 4.11 are crucial to the perception of effects. The ordering of the countries by the country medians establishes gestalts on each panel that are easier to compare from one panel to the next. For example, this allows us to see that the sheep data behave differently from the data of the other livestock types. The amount of variation in the log counts for sheep is greater than that of the other livestock types; in other words, the ordering of the sheep data agrees the least well with the ordering of the country medians. Also, the median ordering of the countries provides a benchmark for each log count — the values of the nearby log counts in the same panel. For example, Figure 4.11 shows that the small log cattle count in Albania is not unusually small given the overall rank of Albania, but the log pig count in Ireland is unusually small given the overall rank of Ireland.

In Figure 4.12, the log counts are displayed again with the levels ordered alphabetically and the panels ordered arbitrarily. Many of the effects readily seen in Figure 4.11 are not revealed. The sheep data no longer stand out as particularly unusual, and we cannot see that the log pig count in Ireland is small or that the log cattle count in Albania fits the pattern of the data.

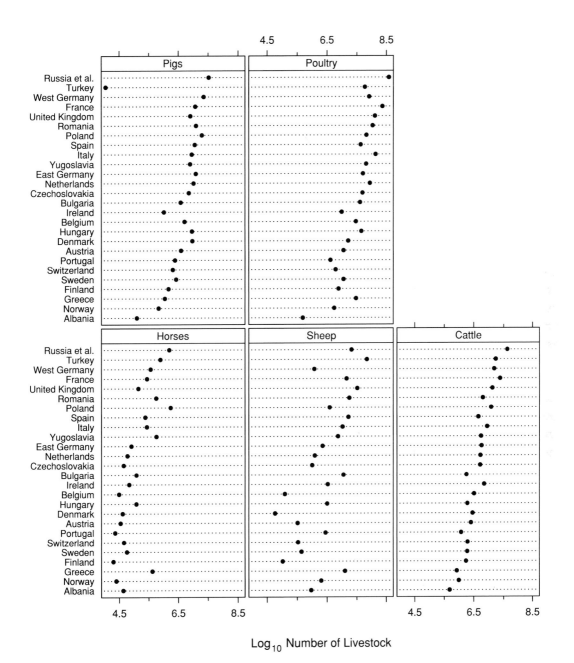

4.11 ORDER FOR MULTIWAY DOT PLOTS. On this multiway dot plot the countries are ordered so that the country medians increase from bottom to top, and the panels are ordered so that the livestock medians increase from left to right and from bottom to top.

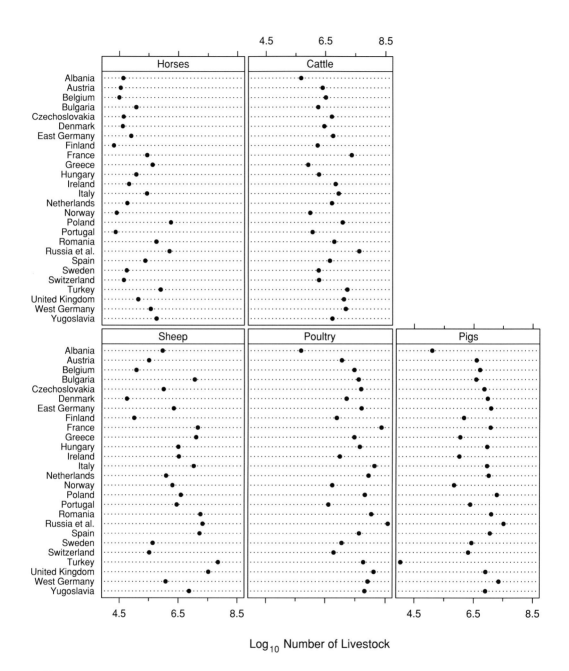

4.12 ORDER FOR MULTIWAY DOT PLOTS. On this multiway dot plot the countries are ordered alphabetically. Properties of the data apparent in Figure 4.11 cannot be seen.

4.7   *Banking to 45°*

Banking to 45°, used extensively in the book, was introduced and discussed in detail in Section 2.4 (pp. 66-79). So was the aspect ratio, which controls banking. Recall that the aspect ratio is the height of the data rectangle divided by its width. This section contains both the studies in graphical perception that led to banking [33,37] and the details of the banking method [26].

Insight, Hypothesis, and Experiment

The issues involved in banking to 45° are intricate and required extensive investigation to confirm hypotheses. But as with many complicated issues, the essential insight is relatively simple.

Consider Figure 4.13. The top left panel shows two line segments with positive unequal slopes. The scale slopes — that is, the slopes of the segments measured in scale units — are 0.75 volts/sec for the upper right segment and 0.33 volts/sec for the lower left segment. The ratio of the larger slope to the smaller is 2.25. The physical slopes — that is, the slopes measured in physical units such as cm — are 1.5 vcm/hcm and 0.67 vcm/hcm where "vcm" means vertical cm and "hcm" means horizontal cm. The ratio of the physical slopes is the same as the ratio of the scale slopes, 2.25.

The *orientations* of the segments are their angles with the horizontal. If θ is the orientation of a segment and s is the physical slope then $s = \tan(\theta)$. We measure orientation in degrees; segments with positive slopes have positive orientations and segments with negative slopes have negative orientations. A segment with a physical slope of 1 vcm/hcm has an orientation of 45° and a segment with a slope of -1 has an orientation of $-45°$. For the two segments in the top left panel of Figure 4.13, the orientations are 56.3° and 33.7°.

The slopes of line segments on a graph encode information about rate of change. For example, the slopes of the local line segments that make up a curve, $y = f(x)$, encode information about the rate of change of y as a function of x. We estimate the orientations of the segments to provide information about the relative rate of change. Thus it is not slope itself we judge but rather a transformation of the slope.

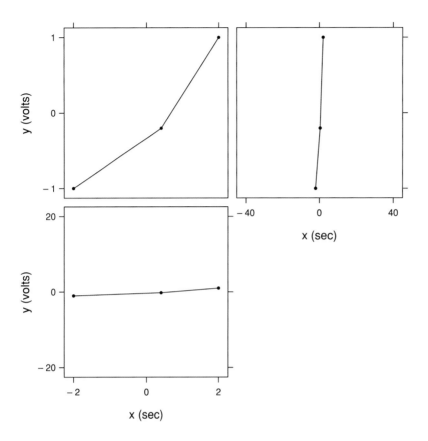

4.13 THE 45° PRINCIPLE. Centering two line segments on 45° maximizes their angular separation, which enhances our judgment of rate of change. In the upper left panel the two segments are centered on 45° in the sense that the average of the two orientations is 45°. In the other panels the aspect ratios are very different from the one that centers the segments on 45°, and the angular separations in both cases are far smaller.

In the right panel of Figure 4.13 the segments are graphed again with a different horizontal scale. The aspect ratio is now very large, the orientations are much steeper, and the difference of the orientations is much smaller. The ratio of the two slopes is the same, so if it were slope that we estimated directly there would be no problem. But we estimate the orientations, and the relationship of the orientations has changed quite substantially. In particular, because the difference of the two orientations is small, it is difficult to discriminate a difference between them; in other words, the slopes appear to be the same or very nearly so. This is a general phenomenon. If the aspect ratio of a display gets too big, we can no longer discriminate two positive slopes or two negative slopes because the orientations get too close. A similar statement holds when the aspect ratio is too small. This is illustrated in the bottom panel of Figure 4.13.

The important insight in banking to 45° was to ask the following question: since the aspect ratio controls the angular separation of two line segments with positive, unequal slopes, what aspect ratio maximizes the absolute difference of their orientations? The answer is the aspect ratio that makes the arithmetic average of the two orientations equal to 45°. Similarly, the absolute difference of the orientations for two segments with negative, unequal slopes is maximized when their average orientation is −45°.

A simple argument proves this 45° principle. We will treat the case of two positive, unequal slopes. Let $\widehat{a}$ be the value of the aspect ratio that makes the average of the two orientations equal to 45°. When the average is 45° each orientation is 90° minus the other, so if $\widehat{s}$ is one of the physical slopes the other is $1/\widehat{s}$ because of the identity

$$\tan(\theta) = 1/\tan(90° - \theta) \, .$$

Suppose it is $\widehat{s}$ that is the bigger of the two slopes. If we multiply the aspect ratio $\widehat{a}$ by a factor f, the new aspect ratio is $a = f\widehat{a}$, the physical slopes are $f\widehat{s}$ and $\widehat{f}/s$, and the difference of the orientations is

$$d(f) = \arctan(f\widehat{s}) - \arctan(f/\widehat{s}) \, .$$

The derivative of d at f is

$$
\begin{aligned}
d'(f) &= \frac{\widehat{s}}{1 + f^2\widehat{s}^2} - \frac{1/\widehat{s}}{1 + f^2/\widehat{s}^2} \\[2mm]
&= \frac{(1 - f^2)(\widehat{s} - 1/\widehat{s})}{(1 + f^2\widehat{s}^2)(1 + f^2/\widehat{s}^2)} \, .
\end{aligned}
$$

$d'(f)$ is positive for $f < 1$, zero for $f = 1$, and negative for $f > 1$. Thus $d(f)$ is a maximum when $f = 1$.

This fact about the absolute difference of orientations led to the 45° hypothesis: the orientations of two line segments with positive slopes are most accurately estimated when the average of the orientations is 45°, and the orientations of two line segments with negative slopes are most accurately estimated when the average of the orientations is −45°.

An experiment was run to confirm the 45° hypothesis. Subjects where shown pairs of line segments and were asked to estimate what percent the slope of one segment was of the other. The experiment unequivocally confirmed the hypothesis.

The Details of Banking to 45°.

The 45° principle applies to the estimation of the slopes of two line segments. But we seldom have just two segments to judge on a display, and the aspect ratio that centers one pair of segments with positive slopes on 45° will not in general center some other pair of segments with positive slopes on 45°. Banking to 45° is a compromise method that centers the absolute values of the orientations of the entire collection of line segments on 45° to enhance overall the estimation of the rate of change.

Let v be the length in physical units of a vertical side of the data rectangle of a graph. Let $\ddot{v}$ be the length of the vertical side in scale units. Similarly, let h be the length in physical units of a horizontal side of the data rectangle, and let $\ddot{h}$ be the length in scale units.

Consider the length of any interval on the vertical scale of a graph. The value $v/\ddot{v}$ is the conversion factor that takes the length in scale units and changes it to a length in physical units on the graph. Similarly, $h/\ddot{h}$ is the conversion factor for the horizontal scale.

The aspect ratio of the data on the graph is

$$a(h, v) = v/h .$$

Suppose the units of the data are fixed so that $\ddot{v}$ and $\ddot{h}$ are fixed values. The values of v and h are under our control in graphing the data, and the aspect ratio is determined by our choices of them.

Consider a collection of n line segments inside the data region. Let $\ddot{v}_i$ be the absolute value of the difference in scale units of the vertical scale values of the two end points of the ith line segment. Let $v_i(v)$ be the absolute difference in physical units when the vertical length of the data rectangle is v. Define $\ddot{h}_i$ and $h_i(h)$ similarly. Let

$$\bar{v}_i = \ddot{v}_i/\ddot{v}$$

and

$$\bar{h}_i = \ddot{h}_i/\ddot{h}\ .$$

The absolute value of the orientation of the ith segment is

$$\theta_i(h, v) = \arctan\left(\frac{v_i(v)}{h_i(v)}\right) = \arctan\left(a(h, v)\bar{v}_i/\bar{h}_i\right)\ .$$

The physical length of the ith segment is

$$\ell_i(h, v) = \sqrt{h_i^2(h) + v_i^2(v)} = h\sqrt{\bar{h}_i^2 + a^2(h, v)\bar{v}_i^2}\ .$$

One method for banking the n segments to $45°$ is to choose $a(h, v)$ so that the mean of the absolute orientations weighted by the line segment lengths is $45°$. (Strictly speaking this does not adhere to the $45°$ principle because the centering solution for two segments derived earlier sets the unweighted average to $45°$, but experimentation with many data sets suggested that the weighted criterion performed somewhat better for the case of many segments, the common one.) Thus

$$\frac{\sum_{i=1}^{n} \theta_i(h, v)\ell_i(h, v)}{\sum_{i=1}^{n} \ell_i(h, v)} = \frac{\sum_{i=1}^{n} \arctan\left(a(h, v)\bar{v}_i/\bar{h}_i\right)\sqrt{\bar{h}_i^2 + a^2(h, v)\bar{v}_i^2}}{\sum_{i=1}^{n} \sqrt{\bar{h}_i^2 + a^2(h, v)\bar{v}_i^2}}$$

is equal to $45°$. Notice that the right side of this formula depends on v and h only through $a(h, v)$. As is intuitively clear, if we multiply v and h by the same factor, the orientations of the segments do not change. Only their ratio matters. Thus it is the aspect ratio that controls banking.

There is no closed-form solution for the aspect ratio that makes the above weighted mean absolute orientation equal to $45°$. The value of a needs to be found by iterative approximation. But the approximation can be fast because the weighted mean is a monotone function of a.

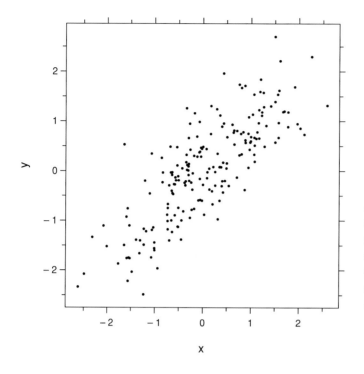

4.15 ESTIMATION OF CORRELATION. Our estimation of correlation is affected by the area of the data rectangle divided by the area of the scale-line rectangle. In this example, the ratio is close to 1.

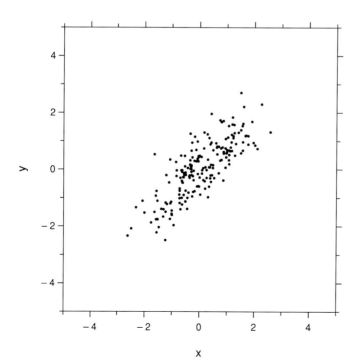

4.16 ESTIMATION OF CORRELATION. The data of Figure 4.15 are graphed again and the area of the data rectangle divided by the area of the scale-line rectangle is much smaller. The amount of correlation now appears greater.

4.9   *Graphing Along a Common Scale*

Figure 4.17, shown earlier in Section 4.6 (pp. 244–250), graphs the logarithms of livestock counts from a census of farm animals in 26 countries. The livestock variable is encoded by the panels and the country variable is encoded by the levels of each panel. The result is that the 26 values for each livestock type are on one panel; the 26 values are encoded by *position along a common scale*. But the five values for each country are graphed on the five panels, one value per panel; that is, they are graphed on *identical but nonaligned scales*.

The consequence of graphing the 26 values for each livestock type along a common scale, but not the five values for each country, is that we can more efficiently decode the values for each livestock type than the values for each country. There are two reasons for this. First, the assembly of values on a single panel is far more efficient. In Figure 4.17 we can effortlessly assemble the values for a particular livestock type, but the assembly of values for a particular country requires a slow sequential search. The second reason is a detection issue. Graphing values along a common scale allows us to detect geometric aspects that contribute substantially to our pattern perception. These aspects are not detectable when the values are graphed on identical, nonaligned scales. Consider the lower left panel in Figure 4.17. Going from the bottom to the top of the panel, the line segments connecting successive dots provide information about the magnitudes of the differences of the successive values. Also, through a visual projective process, we can also compare differences of any two values on the display. For example, to compare the horizontal separation between horses in Poland and horses in Greece, we can visually project the Poland dot down to the dotted line for Greece and then estimate the distance between the Greece dot and the projection.

This asymmetry for a multiway dot plot — better visual decoding for one categorical variable than another — is typically undesirable because we are typically interested equally in the effects of all categorical variables. For example, for the data in Figure 4.17, we are as interested in decoding values for each country as we are in decoding values for each livestock type. The solution is to make as many multiway dot plots as there are categorical variables, with each variable assigned once to the panels. In Figure 4.18 the country variable is assigned to the panels and now we can more effectively judge values for each country.

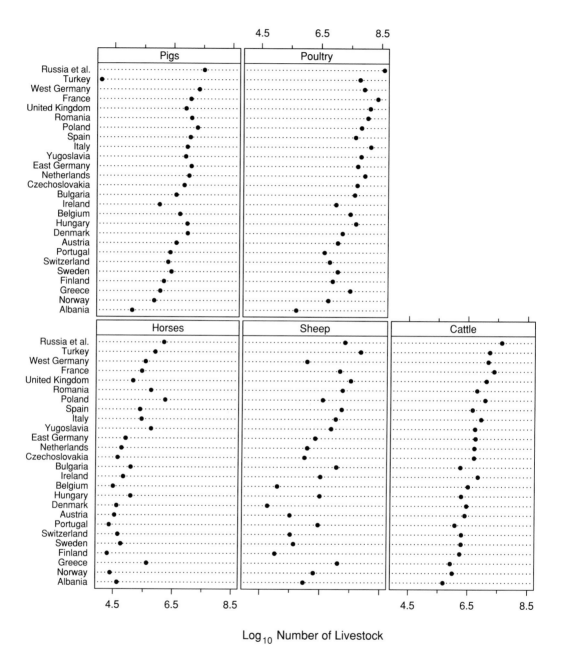

Log$_{10}$ Number of Livestock

4.17 POSITION ALONG A COMMON SCALE. The data for each livestock type are graphed by position along a common scale, which allows us to effectively decode the distribution of the values for each type.

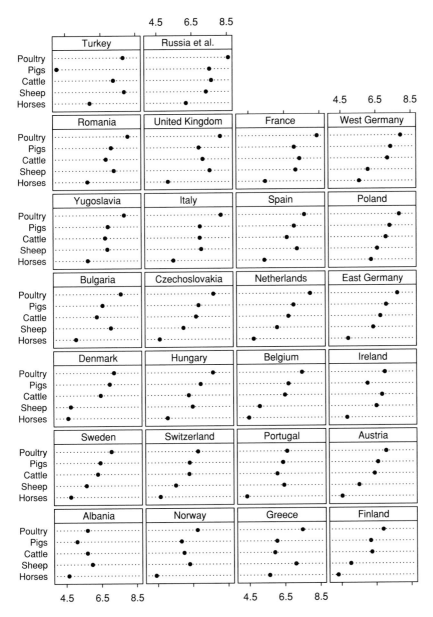

Log$_{10}$ Number of Livestock

4.18 POSITION ALONG A COMMON SCALE. The data for each country are graphed by position along a common scale, which allows us to effectively decode the distribution of the values for each country.

4.10   Pop Charts

Three graphical methods — pie charts, divided bar charts, and area charts — are widely used in mass media and business publications but are used far less in science and technology. Because of their use, we will call these graphical methods *pop charts*.

Any data that can be encoded by one of these pop charts can also be encoded by either a dot plot or a multiway dot plot that typically provides far more efficient pattern perception and table look-up than the pop-chart encoding. Interestingly, the better pattern perception results from a detection operation, a phenomenon that has been missed in previous studies of pop charts.

Pie Charts

Figure 4.19 is a pie chart that graphs 10 percentages. The labels, ten band numbers, are an ordered categorical variable; that is, Band 1 is first, Band 2 is second, and so forth. Kosslyn has argued that the sizes of sectors of a pie-chart encoding should increase circularly [75], just as we have argued in Section 4.6 (pp. 244–250) that categories of dot plots should be ordered so that the numerical values increase from bottom to top. But for our pie-chart example here, since the categories are ordered, we have not ordered the numerical values circularly, just as we do not order dot plots by the numerical values when the categories are ordered.

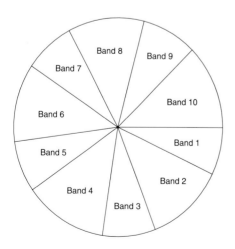

4.19 PIE CHART. The pie chart falls in the category of a pop chart — a graphical method used frequently in the mass media and certain business presentations but far less in science and technology. Both table look-up and pattern perception are less efficient for pie charts than for dot plots.

Figure 4.20 is a dot plot of the ten percentages from Figure 4.19. Pattern perception is far more efficient for this display than for the pie chart. We can effortlessly see a number of properties of the data that are either not apparent at all on the pie chart or are just barely noticeable. First, the percentages have a bimodal distribution; odd numbered bands cluster about 8% and even numbered bands cluster about 12%. Furthermore, the shape of the pattern for the odd values as the band number increases is the same as the shape for the even values; each even value is shifted with respect to the preceding odd value by about 4%.

The poor performance of pattern perception for pie charts is not restricted to cases with ordered labels. Many other simple demonstrations show that the poor performance is pervasive [8,121].

A dot plot graphs data by position along a common scale. As discussed in Section 4.9 (pp. 259–261), one strength of such position encoding is the detection of line segments that provide information about the differences of the graphed values. For example, in Figure 4.20 our ability to detect and cluster the line segments between the odd values and the line segments between the even values results in two gestalts that appear to be horizontal translations of one another, which allows us to readily perceive the 4% shift. There is no corresponding detection operation for the pie chart that allows effortless decoding of differences. The result is degraded pattern perception.

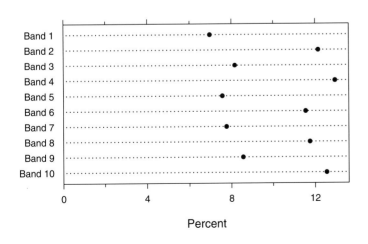

4.20 DOT PLOT. The data from Figure 4.19 are graphed by a dot plot. Patterns emerge that cannot be decoded from Figure 4.19.

This insight about detection has been missed in previous comparisons of pie charts and graphing along a common scale. Many studies treated estimation of the quantities directly graphed as the fundamental issue [36,75,114]. For example, in Figure 4.20 the horizontal line segments from the data dots to the left side of the scale-line rectangle encode the percentages. The studies compared estimation of ratios of such line segments with estimation of ratios of sector sizes of pie charts. Typically, the line segment estimation was found to be more accurate than the sector size estimation, and this was assumed to be the fundamental issue for the poorer pattern perception from pie-chart encodings. But the fundamental issue is the efficient detection of differences of values for position along a common scale; this is the cause of the better estimation observed in the studies.

In other studies it has been argued that the pie chart sometimes provides better estimation of the individual values of the percents [42,109]. The experimental information appears to support this assertion, but the result is largely an artifact of the experimental protocol. The increased accuracies for the pie charts in the experiments occur for percents in the vicinity of 25% and 50% and result from our ability to very accurately judge the sizes of 90° and 180° angles; these values serve as *anchors* [109]. The increase could be eliminated in such experiments simply by drawing reference lines at 25% and 50% on the displays that encode the data by position along a common scale. But more fundamentally, such experiments confuse table look-up with pattern perception. The decoding of individual values in isolation is not a salient visual operation for pattern perception.

Table look-up is also more efficient on dot plots than on pie charts. Most pie charts are drawn with no scales so we must judge the sizes of angles to infer percentages. This is both slower and less accurate than the scanning and interpolation discussed in Section 4.1 (pp. 223–227), which we use to carry out table look-up for data graphed along a common scale. It would be possible to draw a circular scale around a pie chart, but to carry out table look-up would still be slower and less accurate than for a dot plot because it would typically require two scans and interpolations to decode a single value.

Divided Bar Charts

Figure 4.21 is a divided bar chart that shows the percentages of the vote for each of three candidates — Mondale, Hart, and Jackson — in a sample of 2016 voters leaving polling places in the 1984 New York State Democratic primary in the U. S. [117]. There are four age groups and six categories of voters. The percentages for the three candidates do not add to 100 in all cases because of rounding of the reported data, voting for others, or omitted answers.

The Mondale bars in Figure 4.21 all have a common baseline at the left of the graph, and the positions of the right ends of the bars encode the Mondale vote. In other words, the Mondale values are encoded by position along a common scale and we have the benefit of increased detection to judge differences of Mondale values. We cannot do this for the Hart or the Jackson values; neither has a fixed baseline and so the lengths of the bars convey the values, not their positions. Consequently, there is no efficient visual mechanism for detecting differences of values. This reduces the efficiency of pattern perception for the Hart and Jackson values.

Figure 4.22 is a two-way dot plot of the voting data. Now the data for each combination of candidate and voter group are encoded by position along a common scale, not just Mondale. This allows us to perceive patterns in the data that are not apparent in Figure 4.21. For example, we see a Hart age effect. The 30-44 age group is often Hart's strongest; when it was not, the 18-29 age group is usually the strongest. In Figure 4.21 the Hart age effect is not readily apparent.

Table look-up is also far less efficient for divided bar charts than for multiway dot plots. Consider the value for the Hart white vote in the 18-29 age group in Figure 4.22. Scanning and interpolation to the top scale line readily provides a value of about 50%. To decode the same value from Figure 4.21 requires two scans and interpolations which is slower and less accurate.

Area Charts

In 1801, William Playfair published his *Statistical Breviary* [105], which contains many displays of economic and demographic data. On one display Playfair encoded the populations of 22 cities by the areas of circles, although, as we saw in Section 3.2 (pp. 126–132) his encoding had errors as large as ±15%. Playfair may have been the first person to make such an area chart.

Figure 4.23 graphs the Playfair population data by circles whose areas are proportional to the data. As with pie charts and divided bar charts, area charts do not provide efficient detection of geometric objects that convey information about differences of values.

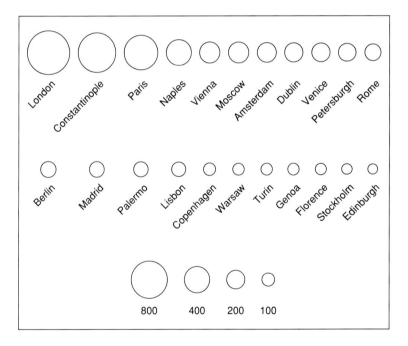

4.23 AREA CHART. Populations of European cities are graphed by an area chart. As with pie charts and divided bar charts, area charts do not have geometric aspects that can be detected to provide information about differences of graphed values.

Figure 4.24 is a dot plot of the population data using a log scale. Now the data are graphed by position along a common scale and pattern perception is far more efficient than in Figure 4.23. For example, it is hard from Figure 4.23 to detect a change in the circle areas from Petersburgh to Lisbon, but Figure 4.24 shows that the populations vary by a large factor.

Table look-up is far more accurate and rapid from Figure 4.24 than from Figure 4.23. The matching operations necessary to decode values from Figure 4.23 are both slower and less accurate than the scanning and interpolation operations that provide table look-up from Figure 4.24.

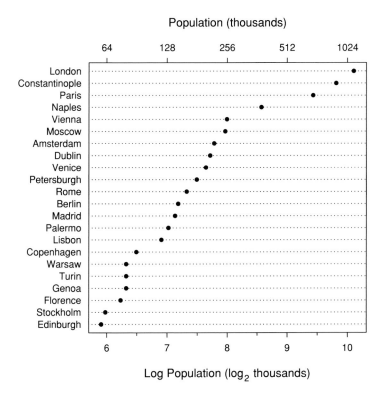

4.24 POSITION JUDGMENTS. The data from Figure 4.23 are graphed by a dot plot with a log scale. Now the data are encoded by position along a common scale and the efficiency of pattern perception and table look-up is much greater.

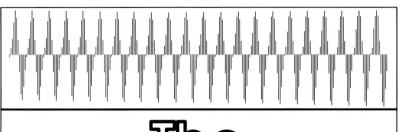

The Elements of Graphing Data

William S. Cleveland

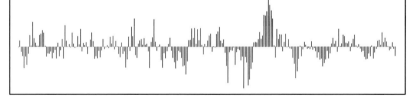

Bibliography

[1] E. A. Abbott. *Flatland; A Romance of Many Dimensions*. Dover Publications, New York, 6th edition, 1952.

[2] L. W. Alvarez, W. Alvarez, F. Asaro, and H. V. Michel. Extraterrestrial Cause for the Cretaceous-Tertiary Extinction. *Science*, 208: 1095–1108, 1980.

[3] R. B. Bacastow, C. D. Keeling, and T. P. Whorf. Seasonal Amplitude in Atmospheric CO_2 Concentration at Mauna Loa, Hawaii, 1959–1980. Paper presented at the Conference on Analysis and Interpretation of CO_2 Data, World Meteorological Organization, Bern, September 14–18, 1981.

[4] J. C. Baird and E. Noma. *Fundamentals of Scaling and Psychophysics*. Wiley, New York, 1978.

[5] R. A. Becker and J. M. Chambers. *S: An Interactive Environment for Data Analysis and Graphics*. Chapman and Hall, New York, 1984.

[6] R. A. Becker and W. S. Cleveland. Brushing Scatterplots. *Technometrics*, 29: 127–142, 1987.

[7] J. L. Bentley, D. S. Johnson, T. Leighton, and C. C. McGeoch. An Experimental Study of Bin Packing. In *Proceedings, Twenty-First Annual Allerton Conference on Communication, Control, and Computing*, pages 51–60. University of Illinois, Urbana-Champaign, Illinois, U.S.A., 1983.

[8] J. Bertin. *Semiologie Graphique*. Gauthier-Villars, Paris, 2nd edition, 1973. (English translation: J. Bertin, *Semiology of Graphics*. University of Wisconsin Press, Madison, Wisconsin, U.S.A., 1983).

[9] T. A. Boden, R. J. Sepanski, and F. W. Stoss. Trends '91: A Compendium of Data on Global Change — Highlights. Technical report, Carbon Dioxide Information Analysis Center, Oak Ridge National Laboratory, Oak Ridge, Tennessee, U.S.A., 1992.

[10] J. H. B. Bridge and J. B. Bassingthwaighte. Uphill Sodium Transport Driven by an Inward Calcium Gradient in Heart Muscle. *Science*, 219: 178–180, 1983.

[11] N. D. Brinkman. Ethanol Fuel — A Single-Cylinder Engine Study of Efficiency and Exhaust Emissions. *SAE Transactions*, 80: 1410–1424, 1981.

[12] W. C. Brinton. *Graphical Methods for Presenting Facts.* Engineering Magazine Co., New York, 1914.

[13] S. M. Bruntz, W. S. Cleveland, B. Kleiner, and J. L. Warner. The Dependence of Ambient Ozone on Solar Radiation, Wind, Temperature, and Mixing Height. In *Symposium on Atmospheric Diffusion and Air Pollution*, pages 125–128. American Meteorological Society, Boston, 1974.

[14] E. Buijsman, H. F. M. Maas, and W. A. H. Asman. Anthropogenic NH_3 Emissions in Europe. *Atmospheric Environment*, 21: 1009–1022, 1987.

[15] C. Burt. Intelligence and Social Mobility. *British Journal of Statistical Psychology*, 14: 3–23, 1961.

[16] J. M. Chambers, W. S. Cleveland, B. Kleiner, and P. A. Tukey. *Graphical Methods for Data Analysis.* Chapman and Hall, New York, 1983.

[17] S. Chatterjee and S. Chatterjee. New Lamps for Old: An Exploratory Analysis of Running Times in Olympic Games. *Applied Statistics*, 31: 14–22, 1982.

[18] A. M. Cheh, J. Skochdopole, P. Koski, and L. Cole. Nonvolatile Mutagens in Drinking Water: Production by Chlorination and Destruction by Sulfite. *Science*, 207: 90–92, 1980.

[19] W. S. Churchill. *The Second World War.* Houghton Mifflin, Boston, 1948–1953.

[20] J. A. P. Clayburn, R. S. Harmon, R. J. Pankhurst, and J. F. Brown. Sr, O, and Pb Isotope Evidence for Origin and Evolution of Etive Igneous Complex, Scotland. *Nature*, 303: 492–497, 1983.

[21] R. B. Cleveland, W. S. Cleveland, J. E. McRae, and I. Terpenning. STL: A Seasonal-Trend Decomposition Procedure Based on Loess. *Journal of Official Statistics*, 6: 3–73, 1990.

[22] W. S. Cleveland. Robust Locally Weighted Regression and Smoothing Scatterplots. *Journal of the American Statistical Association*, 74: 829–836, 1979.

[23] W. S. Cleveland. Graphical Methods for Data Presentation: Full Scale Breaks, Dot Charts, and Multibased Logging. *The American Statistician*, 38: 270–280, 1984.

[24] W. S. Cleveland. Graphs in Scientific Publications. *The American Statistician*, 38: 261–269, 1984.

[25] W. S. Cleveland. A Model for Studying Display Methods of Statistical Graphics (with discussion). *Journal of Computational and Statistical Graphics*, 3: 323–364, 1993.

[26] W. S. Cleveland. *Visualizing Data*. Hobart Press, Summit, New Jersey, U.S.A., 1993.

[27] W. S. Cleveland and S. J. Devlin. Locally-Weighted Regression: An Approach to Regression Analysis by Local Fitting. *Journal of the American Statistical Association*, 83: 596–610, 1988.

[28] W. S. Cleveland, S. J. Devlin, and E. Grosse. Regression by Local Fitting: Methods, Properties, and Computational Algorithms. *Journal of Econometrics*, 37: 87–114, 1988.

[29] W. S. Cleveland, P. Diaconis, and R. McGill. Variables on Scatterplots Look More Highly Correlated When the Scales are Increased. *Science*, 216: 1138–1140, 1982.

[30] W. S. Cleveland, A. Freeny, and T. E. Graedel. The Seasonal Component of Atmospheric CO_2: Information From New Approaches to the Decomposition of Seasonal Time Series. *Journal of Geophysical Research*, 88: 10934–10946, 1983.

[31] W. S. Cleveland, T. E. Graedel, B. Kleiner, and J. L. Warner. Sunday and Workday Variations in Photochemical Air Pollutants in New Jersey and New York. *Science*, 186: 1037–1038, 1974.

[32] W. S. Cleveland and E. Grosse. Computational Methods for Local Regression. *Statistics and Computing*, 1: 47–62, 1991.

[33] W. S. Cleveland, M. E. McGill, and R. McGill. The Shape Parameter of a Two-Variable Graph. *Journal of the American Statistical Association*, 83: 289–300, 1988.

[34] W. S. Cleveland and R. McGill. Graphical Perception: Theory, Experimentation, and Application to the Development of Graphical Methods. *Journal of the American Statistical Association*, 79: 531–554, 1984.

[35] W. S. Cleveland and R. McGill. The Many Faces of a Scatterplot. *Journal of the American Statistical Association*, 79: 807–822, 1984.

[36] W. S. Cleveland and R. McGill. Graphical Perception and Graphical Methods for Analyzing and Presenting Scientific Data. *Science*, 229: 828–833, 1985.

[37] W. S. Cleveland and R. McGill. Graphical Perception: The Visual Decoding of Quantitative Information on Graphical Displays of Data. *Journal of the Royal Statistical Society, Series A*, 150: 192–229, 1987.

[38] W. S. Cleveland and I. J. Terpenning. Graphical Methods for Seasonal Adjustment. *Journal of the American Statistical Association*, 77: 52–62, 1982.

[39] J. Conway. Class Differences in General Intelligence: II. *British Journal of Statistical Psychology*, 12: 5–14, 1959.

[40] F. B. Craves, B. Zalc, L. Leybin, N. Baumann, and H. H. Loh. Antibodies to Cerebroside Sulfate Inhibit the Effects of Morphine and β-Endorphin. *Science*, 207: 75–76, 1980.

[41] G. Crile and D. P. Quiring. A Record of the Body Weight and Certain Organ and Gland Weights of 3690 Animals. *The Ohio Journal of Science*, 15: 219–259, 1940.

[42] F. E. Croxton and R. E. Stryker. Bar Charts Versus Circle Diagrams. *Journal of the American Statistical Association*, 22: 473–482, 1927.

[43] S. R. Dalal, E. B. Fowlkes, and B. Hoadley. Risk Analysis of the Space Shuttle: Pre-Challenger Prediction of Failure. *Journal of the American Statistical Association*, 84: 945–957, 1989.

[44] O. L. Davies, G. E. P. Box, W. R. Cousins, F. R. Himsworth, H. Kenney, M. Milbourn, W. Spendley, and W. L. Stevens. *Statistical Methods in Research and Production*. Hafner, New York, 3rd edition, 1957.

[45] W. E. Deming. Letter to William S. Cleveland, 1985.

[46] D. D. Dorfman. The Cyril Burt Question: New Findings. *Science*, 201: 1177–1186, 1978.

[47] Encyclopaedia Britannica. Meteorites. *Encyclopaedia Britannica*, 15: 272–277, Chicago, 1970.

[48] J. Feynman and N. U. Crooker. The Solar Wind at the Turn of the Century. *Nature*, 275: 626–627, 1978.

[49] W. Fillius, W. H. Ip, and C. E. McIlwain. Trapped Radiation Belts of Saturn: First Look. *Science*, 207: 425–431, 1980.

[50] J. D. Foley, A. van Dam, S. K. Feiner, and J. F. Hughes. *Computer Graphics: Principles and Practice*. Addison-Wesley, Reading, Massachusetts, U.S.A., 1990.

[51] J. P. Frisby and J. L. Clatworthy. Learning to See Complex Random-Dot Stereograms. *Perception*, 4: 173–178, 1975.

[52] S. J. Gould. *Ever Since Darwin: Reflections in Natural History*. Norton, New York, 1977.

[53] S. J. Gould. *Hen's Teeth and Horse's Toes*. Norton, New York, 1983.

[54] S. J. Gould. Dinosaurs in the Haystack. *Natural History*, pages 2–13, March 1992.

[55] J. W. Grier. Ban of DDT and Subsequent Recovery of Reproduction in Bald Eagles. *Science*, 218: 1232–1235, 1982.

[56] R. N. Haber and L. Wilkinson. Perceptual Components of Computer Displays. *IEEE Computer Graphics and Applications*, 2: 23–35, 1982.

[57] J. Hansen, D. Johnson, A. Lacis, S. Lebedeff, P. Lee, D. Rind, and G. Russell. Climate Impact of Increasing Atmospheric Carbon Dioxide. *Science*, 213: 957–966, 1981.

[58] L. S. Hearnshaw. *Cyril Burt, Psychologist*. Cornell University Press, Ithaca, New York, U.S.A., 1979.

[59] A. Hewitt and G. Burbidge. A Revised Optical Catalog of Quasi-Stellar Objects. *The Astrophysical Journal Supplement Series*, 43: 57–158, 1980.

[60] J. C. Houck, C. Kimball, C. Chang, N. W. Pedigo, and H. I. Yamamura. Placental β-Endorphin-Like Peptides. *Science*, 207: 78–80, 1980.

[61] D. Huff. *How to Lie with Statistics*. Norton, New York, 1954.

[62] M. W. Hunkapiller and L. E. Hood. New Protein Sequenator with Increased Sensitivity. *Science*, 207: 523–525, 1980.

[63] F. R. Immer, H. K. Hayes, and L. Powers. Statistical Determination of Barley Varietal Adaption. *Journal of the American Society of Agronomy*, 26: 403–419, 1934.

[64] Z. M. Iqbal, K. Dahl, and S. S. Epstein. Role of Nitrogen Dioxide in the Biosynthesis of Nitrosamines in Mice. *Science*, 207: 1475–1477, 1980.

[65] H. J. Jerison. Brain to Body Ratios and the Evolution of Intelligence. *Science*, 121: 447–449, 1955.

[66] F.-M. Judge, D. L. Wu and R. W. Carlson. Ultraviolet Photometer Observations of the Saturnian System. *Science*, 207: 431–434, 1980.

[67] B. Julesz. Texture in Visual Perception. *Scientific American*, 212(2): 38–48, 1965.

[68] B. Julesz. *Foundations of Cyclopean Perception*. University of Chicago Press, Chicago, 1971.

[69] B. Julesz. Textons, the Elements of Perception, and Their Interactions. *Nature*, 290: 91–97, 1981.

[70] L. Kamin. *The Science and Politics of I.Q.* Erlbaum, Potomac, Maryland, U.S.A., 1974.

[102] G. I. Pearman and P. Hyson. The Annual Variation of Atmospheric CO_2 Concentrations Observed in the Northern Hemisphere. *Journal of Geophysical Research*, 86: 9839–9843, 1981.

[103] A. A. Penzias and R. W. Wilson. A Measurement of Excess Antenna Temperature at 4080 Mc/s. *Astrophysical Journal*, 142: 419–421, 1965.

[104] W. Playfair. *The Commercial and Political Atlas*. William Playfair, London, 1786.

[105] W. Playfair. *Statistical Breviary*. William Playfair, London, 1801.

[106] L. Ramist. Personal communication, 1983.

[107] C. Sagan. *The Dragons of Eden: Speculations on the Evolution of Human Intelligence*. Random House, New York, 1977.

[108] S. H. Schneider. *Global Warming: Are We Entering the Greenhouse Century?* Sierra Club Books, San Francisco, 1989.

[109] D. K. Simkin and R. Hastie. An Information-Processing Analysis of Graph Perception. *Journal of the American Statistical Association*, 82: 454–465, 1987.

[110] E. J. Smith, L. Davis, Jr., D. E. Jones, P. J. Coleman, Jr., D. S. Colburn, P. Dyal, and C. P. Sonett. Saturn's Magnetic Field and Magnetosphere. *Science*, 207: 407–410, 1980.

[111] E. M. Smith, W. J. Meyer, and J. E. Blalock. Virus-Induced Corticosterone in Hypophysectomized Mice: A Possible Lymphoid Adrenal Axis. *Science*, 218: 1311–1312, 1982.

[112] R. D. Snee. Experimenting with a Large Number of Variables. In R. D. Snee, editor, *Experiments in Industry*, pages 25–35. American Society for Quality Control, Milwaukee, Wisconsin, U.S.A., 1985.

[113] I. Spence and S. Lewandowsky. Graphical Perception. In J. Fox and S. Long, editors, *Modern Methods of Data Analysis*, pages 13–57. Sage Publications, Beverly Hills, California, U.S.A., 1990.

[114] I. Spence and S. Lewandowsky. Displaying Proportions and Percentages. *Applied Cognitive Psychology*, 5: 61–77, 1991.

[115] W. Strunk, Jr. and E. B. White. *The Elements of Style*. Macmillan, New York, 3rd edition, 1979.

[116] M. Stuiver and P. D. Quay. Changes in Atmospheric Carbon-14 Attributed to a Variable Sun. *Science*, 207: 11–19, 1980.

[117] The New York Times Company. The New York Times/CBS NEWS POLL. *The New York Times*, page B10, April 5, 1984.

[118] J. H. Trainor, F. B. McDonald, and A. W. Schardt. Observations of Energetic Ions and Electrons in Saturn's Magnetosphere. *Science*, 207: 421–425, 1980.

[119] D.T. Travis. *Effective Color Displays: Theory and Practice*. Academic Press, New York, 1991.

[120] A. Treisman. Features and Objects in Visual Processing. *Scientific American*, 255(5): 114B–125, 1986.

[121] E. R. Tufte. *The Visual Display of Quantitative Information*. Graphics Press, Cheshire, Connecticut, U.S.A., 1983.

[122] E. R. Tufte. *Envisioning Information*. Graphics Press, Cheshire, Connecticut, U.S.A., 1990.

[123] J. W. Tukey. *Exploratory Data Analysis*. Addison-Wesley, Reading, Massachusetts, U.S.A., 1977.

[124] P. A. Tukey and J. W. Tukey. Graphical Display of Data Sets in 3 or More Dimensions. In V. Barnett, editor, *Interpreting Multivariate Data*, pages 189–275. Wiley, Chichester, U. K., 1981.

[125] R. P. Turco, O. B. Toon, T. P. Ackerman, J. B. Pollack, and C. Sagan. Nuclear Winter: Global Consequences of Multiple Nuclear Explosions. *Science*, 222: 1283–1292, 1983.

[126] U.S. Bureau of the Census. *Historical Statistics of the United States: Colonial Times to 1970. Bicentennial Edition Part 2*. U.S. Government Printing Office, Washington, D. C., 1975.

[127] U.S. Bureau of the Census. *Statistical Abstract of the United States: 1982–1983*. U.S. Government Printing Office, Washington, D. C., 1982.

[128] U.S. Bureau of the Census. *1980 Census of Population. Volume 1, Characteristics of the Population*. U.S. Government Printing Office, Washington, D. C., 1983.

[129] B. M. Vetter. Working Women Scientists and Engineers. *Science*, 207: 28–34, 1980.

[130] M. Wahlen, C. O. Kunz, J. M. Matuszek, W. E. Mahoney, and R. C. Thompson. Radioactive Plume from the Three Mile Island Accident: Xenon-133 in Air at a Distance of 375 Kilometers. *Science*, 207: 639–640, 1980.

[131] S. Webb and C. S. Cox. Pressure and Electric Fluctuations on the Deep Seafloor: Background Noise for Seismic Detection. *Geophysical Research Letters*, 11: 967–970, 1984.

[132] M. B. Wilk and R. Gnanadesikan. Probability Plotting Methods for the Analysis of Data. *Biometrika*, 55: 1–17, 1968.

[133] N. Yagi and I. Matsubara. Myosin Heads do not Move on Activation in Highly Stretched Vertebrate Striated Muscle. *Science*, 207: 307–308, 1980.

[134] F. Yates. The Design and Analysis of Factorial Experiments. *Imperial Bureau of Soil Science Technical Committee*, 35: 4–95, 1937.

Figure Acknowledgements

Figure 1.3 republished with permission from [31]. Copyright ©1974 by the AAAS.

Figure 1.6 republished from *The Dragons of Eden: Speculations on the Evolution of Human Intelligence*, by Carl Sagan, p. 39. Copyright ©1977 by Carl Sagan. Reprinted by permission of Random House, Inc.

Figure 2.3 republished with permission from [74]. Copyright ©1980 by the AAAS.

Figure 2.5 republished with permission from [20]. Copyright ©1983 by Macmillan Journals Limited.

Figure 2.7 republished with permission from [10]. Copyright ©1983 by the AAAS.

Figure 2.9 republished with permission from [85]. Copyright ©1981 by the AAAS.

Figure 2.11 republished with permission from [62]. Copyright ©1980 by the AAAS.

Figure 2.12 republished with permission from [133]. Copyright ©1980 by the AAAS.

Figure 2.14 republished with permission from [118]. Copyright ©1980 by the AAAS.

Figure 2.16 republished with permission from [76]. Copyright ©1980 by the AAAS.

Figure 2.18 republished from *The Dragons of Eden: Speculations on the Evolution of Human Intelligence*, by Carl Sagan, p. 26. Copyright ©1977 by Carl Sagan. Reprinted by permission of Random House, Inc.

Figure 2.22 republished from *The Dragons of Eden: Speculations on the Evolution of Human Intelligence*, by Carl Sagan, p. 39. Copyright ©1977 by Carl Sagan. Reprinted by permission of Random House, Inc.

Figure 2.25 republished with permission from [130]. Copyright ©1980 by the AAAS.

Figure 2.27 republished with permission from [18]. Copyright ©1980 by the AAAS.

Figure 2.28 republished with permission from [91]. Copyright ©1980 by the AAAS.

Figure 2.29 republished with permission from [49]. Copyright ©1980 by the AAAS.

Figure 2.30 republished with permission from [60]. Copyright ©1980 by the AAAS.

Figure 2.31 republished with permission from [94]. Copyright ©1983 by the IEEE.

Figure 2.33 republished with permission from [133]. Copyright ©1980 by the AAAS.

Figure 2.34 republished with permission from [40]. Copyright ©1980 by the AAAS.

Figure 2.35 republished with permission from [64]. Copyright ©1980 by the AAAS.

Figure 2.37 republished with permission from [110]. Copyright ©1980 by the AAAS.

Figure 2.38 republished with permission from [129]. Copyright ©1980 by the AAAS.

Figure 2.49 republished with permission from [116]. Copyright ©1980 by the AAAS.

Figure 2.57 republished from *How to Lie with Statistics* by Darrell Huff and Irving Geis, p. 65. Copyright ©1954 and renewed 1982 by Darrell Huff and Irving Geis. Reprinted by permission of W. W. Norton & Company, Inc.

Figure 2.58 republished with permission from [66]. Copyright ©1980 by the AAAS.

Figure 2.62 republished from *Their Finest Hour* by Winston S. Churchill, p. 338, 339, 319, 340. Copyright ©1949 by Houghton Mifflin Co. Copyright ©1977 by Lady Spencer-Churchill, The Honourable Lady Sarah Audley, and The Honourable Lady Somes. Reprinted by permission of Houghton Mifflin Co.

Figure 2.69 republished with permission from [101]. Copyright ©1984 by the AAAS.

Figure 2.71 republished with permission from [87]. Copyright ©1980 by the AAAS.

Figure 2.72 republished with permission from [111]. Copyright ©1982 by the AAAS.

Figure 4.6 republished with permission from [88]. Copyright ©1990 by the Optical Society of America.

Colophon

Text and Graphics Layout

The layout of the book is unusual. There are two criteria that override everything else. First, a block of text discussing a graphical display needs to be as close as possible to the display, preferably on the same page or on a facing page. Second, it is vital to make content the master of design and not vice versa. Some approach text-display layout by writing to the design. This typically interferes with the coherence of the discussion. Throwing in a thought because space needs to be filled is not a good way to communicate. The design here solves the layout problem by giving up on filling and balancing pages, a convention thought to be inviolate by some. The spacing between paragraphs and the ragged-right text is meant to lessen the sense of visual order so that the lack of balance and fill is less salient.

Visualization Software Credits

The workhorse software of the book is S, the powerful system developed by Richard Becker, John Chambers, and Allan Wilks. The original visualizations of data that formed the basis of the writing were done in S.

The final rendering of the displays for publication, however, used a number of systems. Except for the color plots in Figures I and II, all final rendering was done by proprietary software of MEM Research, Inc., written by Robert McGill. The software, which is based on S, enables very delicate control of the details of graphs so that graphical elements — such as labels, tick marks, and the positioning of the panels of multi-panel displays — can be placed precisely where they best serve the visualization. The placement was carried out by Marylyn McGill of MEM with enormous attention to detail. The final product was PostScript$^{®}$ files.

The color scatterplot in Figure I was drawn in Adobe Illustrator. The color level plot in Figure II was drawn by S and then moved to Abobe Photoshop for the assignment of CMYK colors to the levels.

The figures that are reproductions of displays from other publications were scanned and then converted to PostScript® files.

Production

This book was typeset in LATEX. The main text is set in palatino, figure legends in helvetica, italics in times, and mathematical symbols in computer modern. Camera-ready copy was produced at AT&T Bell Laboratories on a Linotronic 200 P with a resolution of 1270 dpi.

Edwards Brothers, Inc., of Ann Arbor, Michigan, U.S.A., printed the book. The paper is 70 pound Sterling Satin, the pages are Smythe sewn, and the book is covered with Arrestox®linen.

Index